Including a Special Tribute to John Paul II

A Year in The Life

Volume I

By D.B. Prehoda

Meditations on the Blessed Virgin Mary to Pentecost offered by
Father Richard G. Lavalley, Father Gerald Ragis,
and Reverend De Porres Durham OP

ALSO BY D.B. PREHODA

West of the Moon

UnCivil Servants

The Trail's End

My Life As I Knew It

Published by Stoney Hill Farm Press

Dewey Decimal Classification: 240
Subject Heading: Religion

Scripture readings at the beginning of each chapter were recorded and transcribed during the 2005 calendar year as presented to the Saint Francis Xavier community by the Oregon Catholic Press Missal, used by permission, all rights reserved.

Library of Congress Cataloging-in-Publication Data
Prehoda, D. B., 1960-
     A Year in The Life / D. B. Prehoda

ISBN 978-0-9762428-1-9

Produced and arranged by C.L. Mayer

Edited by Marie-Jose Y. Cartau

Dedication

Foremost, this volume is dedicated to Lucy, Mary, Yvette, Claire, Diane, Maureen, Fran, Laura, Kay, Vicki, Bruce, Clem, and Paul... collectively known as the Saint Francis Xavier Choir, at the time of this writing. A more fitting passage than the one found in Genesis 12:2 there could not be. *" '...I will bless you... and you will be a blessing.' "*

However, as I am want to do with all my writings, I further dedicate this book to my wife, Kathryn, who held my hand as we took our first timid steps across the threshold and through the massive oak doors of Saint Francis Xavier... and into the blessed world of Father Richard G. Lavalley.

Et finalement... je dédié ce livre à mon oncle, Jean-Francois, Le Haou de Roudge, Garlin, France, auteur et aquarelliste, dont j'admire le courage et la fortitude en face des vicissitudes quotidiennes auxquelles il doit faire face et surmonter suivant son transplant cardiaque voila plus de quinze ans passes. Sa joie de vivre est contagieuse, se lit dans ses yeux bruns et vifs, et se manifeste dans ces histoires merveilleuses et colorees dont il aime nous regaler autour de table familliale.

Table of Contents

Chapter	Title	Page
	Preface	1
Chapter I	Blessed Virgin Mary	5
Chapter II	Epiphany of the Lord	15
Chapter III	Baptism of the Lord	25
Chapter IV	Second Sunday in Ordinary Time	37
Chapter V	Third Sunday in Ordinary Time	47
Chapter VI	Fourth Sunday in Ordinary Time	57
Chapter VII	Fifth Sunday in Ordinary Time	69
Chapter VIII	Ash Wednesday	77
Chapter IX	First Sunday of Lent	81
Chapter X	Second Sunday of Lent	93
Chapter XI	Third Sunday of Lent	107
Chapter XII	Fourth Sunday of Lent	119
Chapter XIII	Fifth Sunday of Lent	129
Chapter XIV	Palm Sunday of the Lord's Passion	139
Chapter XV	Holy Thursday, Evening of the Lord's Supper	151
Chapter XVI	Good Friday of the Lord's Passion	157
Chapter XVII	Stations of the Cross	171
Chapter XVIII	Easter Vigil	207
Chapter XIX	Easter Sunday, the Resurrection of the Lord	217
Chapter XX	Second Sunday of Easter	225
Chapter XXI	Third Sunday of Easter Devine Mercy Sunday	237
Chapter XXII	Fourth Sunday of Easter	247
Chapter XXIII	Fifth Sunday of Easter	253
Chapter XXIV	Sixth Sunday of Easter	261
Chapter XXV	Ascension of the Lord	269
Chapter XXVI	Seventh Sunday of Easter	275
Chapter XXVII	Vigil of Pentecost	283
Chapter XXVIII	Pentecost Sunday	291
	A Note from the Scribe	297
	A Tribute to John Paul II	303

Preface

In the truest sense, *A Year in The Life* is love's harvest. It is a body of work that speaks to the overflowing love the shepherd has for his flock; about the purest love the scribe has for the shepherd; about the unconditional love our Lord and Savior Jesus Christ has for all of humanity. It is a body of work that speaks of hope and of love and of the beautiful mystery of our faith.

Traditionally, the residents of Winooski, Vermont, made one of two choices when it came to the celebration of their Catholic faith: Saint Stephens on Barlow Street, for the denizens of the city's east side, or Saint Francis Xavier on St. Peter Street, for those who lived on the west side of the city.

My wife was born and raised in Winooski, and though her immediate family lived on the west side of the city, they worshiped at Saint Stephens. I expect there were several reasons why this came to pass... not the least of which, I suspect, was the fact that the parish of Saint Stephens was thought of, in those days, as being less rigid than was the parish of Saint Francis Xavier.

Whereas, the parish of Saint Francis Xavier possesses a French-Canadian heritage... the parish of Saint Stephens catered to Anglophiles. Whereas, the parish of Saint Francis Xavier possesses magnificent steeples that tower above the city, beckoning those not faint of heart or spirit to enter through its massive oak doors... the parish of Saint Stephens is nestled comfortably just above the banks of the Winooski River, and its marble facade seems less imposing and more accommodating to the casual Catholic. Whereas, it was said, (back in those days), that the fellow over at Saint Francis Xavier took his vocation a bit more seriously than most... Saint Stephens had Father Bombardier.

Father Bombardier was a lighthearted "Friar Tuck" of a priest. He had a generously round belly, a gleam in his eyes, and a smile ready to play out upon his lips. Were it not for the collar of the priest he wore, one could easily have imagined Father Bombardier masquerading as a mischievous imp. He was easy to converse with... comfortable to be around... and was filled with love for his parishioners, his calling, and our Lord and Savior Jesus Christ. Father Bombardier baptized two of my five children. Father Bombardier departed this life on September 03, 2000. He is missed by many of us even to this day.

Conventional wisdom was that the priest over at Saint Francis Xavier was quite the serious fellow... not at all jovial like Father Bombardier. I recall hearing of these rumors and despite the fact that my wife and I lived with our children, and my mother-in-law, at 177 North Street, on the west side of Winooski, such rumors made me more determined than ever not to shorten my semi-annual trek to Sunday worship services. Truth be known, I was one of "those" Catholics you often encounter 'round about Christmastime and Easter... and I was not looking for one of those famous Catholic guilt trips to be laid upon me by a "serious" Scripture scholar.

In those days, I was convinced that I could do it all myself. I could confess my transgressions directly to God... I could receive His absolution without an intermediary... I could interpret Scripture without a teacher, without a mentor... I could celebrate mass once in a blue moon and still reap the benefits known, heretofore, by those "hapless" souls who made Sunday worship a central focus of their spiritual lives... and of the Holy Eucharist, I had convinced myself that such was a ritualistic celebration of *The Last Supper*, not the true presence of Christ in our church, in our midst, in ourselves.

How foolishly naive I was. How terribly wrongheaded were my beliefs...

One Sunday in the fall of '99, my wife and I felt Saint Francis Xavier beckon us... and what could only be explained, at that time, as a momentary lapse of reason, we traveled the few short blocks from our home to Saint Francis Xavier's magnificent oak doors. Taking my wife's hand in mine, more for strength and comfort than intimacy, I timidly crossed the threshold of Saint Francis Xavier and into the life of Father Richard G. Lavalley. I have not been the same man since.

To the parishioners of Saint Francis Xavier, the latter statement is not an anomaly. The parishioners of Saint Francis Xavier know full well the treasure they possess that takes the form of Father Lavalley. Father Lavalley is a man of deep spiritual substance. He is a man possessive of a deep, abiding love for the people whom he serves, for his blessed calling to the priesthood, for everything that is Jesus Christ and is of Jesus Christ. Father Lavalley is a teacher to his people... a mentor to those who thirst for his wisdom. Father Lavalley is a conscience for those who would go astray. He is a comforting shoulder... a steadying hand for those in despair.

In the beginning paragraph of this preface, I spoke of a shepherd who possesses unconditional love for his flock; I spoke of a shepherd for whom I possess the greatest respect and the purist love. I acknowledge the fact that our Lord and Savior Jesus Christ is the Shepherd of all mankind. I delight and take comfort in knowing that one day the loving arms of the Shepherd will encircle me and will welcome me into His home... into my home. But... the shepherd of whom I spoke at the beginning is Father Richard G. Lavalley.

Father Lavalley is truly one of God's shepherds here on earth. I am so honored and so blest to find myself in the midst of his flock.

A Year in The Life is a celebration of the wisdom and compassion of Father Richard G. Lavalley. _A Year in The Life_ is a gift from Father Lavalley to you via my humble fingertips and keystrokes.

It is safe, perhaps, to suggest that Father Lavalley is every bit as mortal as the rest of us who love him so. And so knowing... it follows that his physical manifestation will one day fade from our midst and we will be left feeling adrift and without his steadying hand. What I had hoped to achieve by my scribing of *A Year in The Life* was a lasting legacy, so that your children and mine... my grandchildren and yours... might one day come to know and love the man who has guided, taught, comforted, and loved the parishioners of Saint Francis Xavier for so many years- as we have known and loved him.

There remains little else for me to say at this point other than this: ***Thank-you Father Lavalley for all you have done... for all that you do... for all that will be done by you. May the countenance of our Lord and Savior Jesus Christ continue to shine from you, around you, and within you all the days of your life.***

D.B. Prehoda

Blessed Virgin Mary, Mother of God

A reading from the Book of Numbers:

The Lord said to Moses: "Speak to Aaron and his sons and tell them: This is how you shall bless the Israelites. Say to them: The Lord bless you and keep you! The Lord let his face shine upon you, and be gracious to you! The Lord look upon you kindly and give you peace! So shall they invoke my name upon the Israelites, and I will bless them."

A reading from the Letter of Saint Paul to the Galatians:

Brothers and sisters: When the fullness of time had come, God sent his Son, born of a woman, born under the law, to ransom those under the law, so that we might receive adoption as sons. As proof that you are sons, God sent the Spirit of his Son into our hearts, crying out, "Abba, Father!" So you are no longer a slave but a son, and if a son then also an heir, through God.

A reading from the holy Gospel according to Luke:

The shepherds went in haste to Bethlehem and found Mary and Joseph, and the infant lying in the manger. When they saw this, they made known the message that had been told them about this child. All who heard it were amazed by what had been told them by the shepherds. And Mary kept all these things, reflecting on them in her heart. Then the shepherds returned, glorifying and praising God for all they had heard and seen, just as it had been told to them.

When eight days were completed for his circumcision, he was named Jesus, the name given to him by the angel before he was conceived in the womb.

What are we going to do?

That is a question we ask ourselves many times. We ask it in a variety of settings and in different ways, but the questions begging its answer are similar.

What are we going to do?

Children ask a form of that question when they go to the house of a playmate. "What do we want to do?"

"I don't know. What do you want to do?"

People ask that question when tragedy befalls them.

"What are we going to do?"

When a loved one dies and our world is forced to become reorientated, we ask ourselves, "What are we going to do?"

I believe, if we are honest with ourselves, we would have to admit that on some level there is a little heretic in each of us, because most of us are probably semi-Pelagians at best... and maybe even Pelagians, at worst.

Now... you might be saying to yourself, "I have no idea what that is... I have no idea what a Pelagian is."

A Pelagian is one who believes Christians earn their salvation... that good works open the gates of Heaven to them.

Such belief was one of the very first heresies the Church condemned... the belief that our good works bore us salvation. Such a belief was condemned. Such a belief was wrong. To believe in such a theology would lead you astray.

I submit to you that most of us are semi-Pelagians at best, because I believe a multitude of us go through life with the following image of salvation:

Weighted scales assigned to us when we get to heaven. On one side of the scale our good deeds will be represented, and on the other side our bad deeds will rest. Whichever way the scale tilts will determine our fate.

From the very beginning, the Church's position on such a depiction of salvation was that, (in light of the teachings of Jesus Christ), such a belief is absolutely wrong. We are saved in one way... and only one thing is necessary for our salvation. We are saved, because God freely gives salvation. There is no price. There is no cost. There is nothing to do. It has all been done.

It was done by our Lord and Savior, Jesus Christ.

I mention this, because we often feel as though we are left with many things to do. We look around our world and we ask, "How are we going to do all of the things that need to be done?"

We ask ourselves that question, because we live in a broken world. People around the world are dying from war, famine, and disease. It does not appear that war or human suffering will end anytime soon.

In the not-so-distant past, the peoples of the nations of our world bore witness to several terrible and incomprehensible natural disasters. Many lives were destroyed by a terrible tsunami that struck Indonesia, Sri Lanka, Thailand, and India. Many lives were destroyed by a massive hurricane that struck the Gulf Coast of the United States. Millions of people were made homeless and hundreds of thousands of people were killed.

Obviously, I have no way of knowing if any of you had seen the pictures on television of the devastation wrought by those natural disasters, but I know I was most struck by the before and after satellite photographic images of the devastated areas; to see exactly how much had been ripped up and taken away. While viewing those images, I reflected that it was almost as if God had taken an eraser and had rubbed out the coastlines of the affected countries. Many of those countries were already struggling with much human suffering borne of poverty and war.

Despite our charge as caretakers of this planet, we still cannot, or will not, feed all the peoples of the world. There are corners of our world where thousands of people die each day, because they do not get enough to eat. They die because of some indigenous pathogen. A simple, common, cold virus kills them... or they starve to death.

Look at our own country. We are such a wealthy nation. The argument could be made that we are the wealthiest nation on the planet. Yet, not every citizen has health care. We have not learned how to share with one another. We steal from one another. We kill one another.

The argument could be made that there is no moral compass for many in our country. We kill the most vulnerable among us. We kill the unborn. We encourage the killing of those who are nearing the end of their life, those who are frail, those whose spirit is laid low.

What are we going to do?

That is the wrong question to ask; especially as we celebrate this day, the solemnity of Mary, the mother of God.

In today's Gospel reading, the shepherds went to Bethlehem after having had a miraculous vision of angels. A vision of angels who spoke to them saying, *"Today to you is born a savior, in the city of David. A savior Christ the Lord."*

They go and they visit this message upon Mary. What does Mary do? What does Joseph do?

Joseph is not even mentioned in today's Gospel reading... but I suspect Joseph was like Mary in those days. On the other hand, perhaps Joseph was more like me.

You see... if I were in a situation similar to their's, after having had all of their miraculous experiences - Mary had the physical experience of the angel, Joseph had the experience of an angel in a dream, the shepherds had the experience of an angel of the Lord - I would find myself saying, "I have been entrusted with the son of God, the second person of the blessed Trinity... it would not be good if I screwed this up."

And so, I would begin to worry, "What should I be doing as a parent of the Son of God?"

"How should I raise this child whose birth is so miraculous?"

But Mary and Joseph do not worry about what they are going to do. Such is not even the response of Mary to this profound responsibility. Mary does not ask, "What am I going to do?" To the contrary, we learn from our reading of the Gospel that *...she kept all these things reflecting on them with her heart.*

What are we going to do?

That is the wrong question to ask of ourselves. To formulate the correct question we need to turn to the Gospel and to ask ourselves the question posed by our Lady, to herself.

The question posed by Mary is not "What am I going to do?" but "Who am I?"

Who am I?

I am a disciple. I call the Lord.

The Lord is the one who needs to worry about what we are going to do. We simply need to open ourselves to what God is going to do for us. Mary understood this; that is why she never sinned. Mary did not worry about what she was going to do first. Mary worried first about who she was. Mary was a daughter of God. Mary was open to God. Mary said "yes" to God. Her faith was complete, and total, and entirely. Mary believed in God... and everything she had either came from God or edified God. Throughout her life, Mary brought new questions to God. She brought new experiences to God... she did all of this in an effort to figure out what it meant to follow God with her life.

Saint Thomas Aquinas was once asked, "What type of life is the best life?"

Now, Saint Thomas Aquinas was a Dominican, so it should not come as any great surprise to you that his answer was: "Well, the best way of life is to be a Dominican."

The good news in his response is that it opens a door for us to a life that Saint Thomas Aquinas believed to be the best way of life for all of us.

Dominicans have laity who are married and who are contemplative... but still they are laity. Dominicans have nuns. Dominicans have active sisters; they have brothers; they have priests. Dominicans cover all of the religious bases, if you will. You have a place in Saint Thomas Aquinas' response, and that is the good news; that is why I am sharing it with you.

Why did Saint Thomas Aquinas believe that the Dominican's way of life was the best way to live one's life?

Because of who the Dominicans were. Because of who the Dominicans are, today.

When Dominic de Guzman founded the Order of the Preachers, (the Dominicans), at the beginning of the 13th century, essentially there were two paths one could take towards becoming a priest or a holy person. One way was to live in "community", as a Benedictine monk did, and the other way was to become a "canon regular".

A Benedictine was committed wholly to one monastery. A Benedictine did manual labor in the fields and prayed at regular intervals during the day. "*To work and to pray*" is the motto of the Benedictines, but a Benedictine's life was committed to one monastery. Even to this day Benedictines pledge a vow of stability.

A Canon Regular lived by a rule, whereby, one's whole life was committed to one church; sacraments were administered and prayers were recited at regular intervals throughout the day.

Dominic de Guzman's philosophy of life was to embrace a contemplative lifestyle. A contemplative lifestyle is a wonderful lifestyle. We should all live it. It is a wonderful thing. People should come together at regular times during the day to pray for the betterment of their community. At regular intervals people should reflect and contemplate deeply on God.

The underpinning of a contemplative lifestyle is that contemplation will overflow into positive and productive action. And that is the difference. A contemplative lifestyle is not just a lifestyle of being busy about many things. It is a lifestyle of reflection and contemplation on the presence of God, in all things, and of doing something to let the world know that God is present in the world.

Saint Thomas Aquinas recognized that many people are busy about many things in a good way. If you are raising a family you are busy about many things. You have to be. It is part of your vocation. You might be sent to jail if you are not busy about many things... for neglect, to name but one. You should be busy about many things if you are a parent.

Saint Thomas Aquinas believed that it would be better to live in a moment. Not everybody does, of course, because of the different vocations given to each of us by God. But would it not be wonderful if all of us would set aside moments throughout our busy lives, each day, to reflect on the beauty and presence of God in the world.

God is everywhere... that is what the Scripture makes known to us.

Saint Thomas Aquinas believed it would be better for us if, after having contemplated on the wonderful and tremendous presence of God in our world, we actually did something to let people know that God is present in the world.

And, therein is found the smallest of twists: ***We do something to let the world know that God is present in the world.***

We do not make God present in the world. We participate in what God is doing in our world.

In today's Gospel reading, that is precisely on what our Lady was reflecting. Mary is going to get to work after this particular Gospel passage is concluded. She does many things after this one thing, but the beginning of her new life is contemplation.

I would suggest to you that in our world these days, when we are so overwhelmed with images of people who have died... those who are homeless... those who have so little... those who do not have anything, we should choose to speak of God's love, as one Asian firefighter chose to do when he was interviewed by a member of the international news media following the incomprehensible tragedy visited upon the shores of his country.

He was a firefighter, nameless to all of us except those who knew him in his native land, who had been called away to put out a fire... and while he was fighting that fire... his entire family was swept out to sea by a tsunami that had just devastated the coast of Indonesia. And while he was quoted by one translator as saying, "I don't know what I am going to do", he was also quoted as affirming his belief in the love of God.

Another person, present at the interview, posed the following question to the firefighter, "How can you speak of the love of God in the face of such horrific tragedy?"

I do not recall how that question was answered by the firefighter, but do know we can speak of the love of God, in the face of such unimaginable tragedy, by imitating our Lady and by reflecting on God's presence in our world.

I do not pretend to have answers to explain why such horrible tragedies are visited upon the peoples of this world, but I do know of the close presence of God. And that is what we celebrate this Christmas season. God became human.

God could have given up on us two-thousand years ago. God in His justice could have said, "You screwed up... too bad for you. You had your chance and you blew it."

But He did not.

Not only did God not give up on us, but God entered into a mysterious and beautiful paradox with us. Because God is both a God of justice and a God of mercy... Jesus got the justice... we got the mercy. Jesus paid the price for us. Payment for this price began by Him following the example of His mother, who reflected on who she was... not on what she was going to do.

As we begin this new year, faced with so many new obstacles and so many unimagined challenges, perhaps we could open our hearts... to be contemplative... to follow the example of our Lady; treasuring deeply the signs of God's presence in a world so very broken, so that we might become like the shepherds returning... glorifying... and praising God for all we have heard and seen. God, indeed, is one of us... alive and active in our midst.

Fr. De Porres

We believe in one God, the Father, the Almighty, maker of heaven and earth, of all that is seen and unseen....

Epiphany of the Lord

A reading from the Book of the Prophet Isaiah:

Rise up in splendor, Jerusalem! Your light has come, the glory of the Lord shines upon you. See, darkness covers the earth, and thick clouds cover the peoples; but upon you the Lord shines, and over you appears his glory. Nations shall walk by your light, and kings by your shining radiance. Raise your eyes and look about; they all gather and come to you: your sons come from afar, and your daughters in the arms of their nurses. Then you shall be radiant at what you see, your heart shall throb and overflow, for the riches of the sea shall be emptied out before you, the wealth of nations shall be brought to you. Caravans of camels shall fill you, dromedaries from Midian and Ephah; all from Sheba shall come bearing gold and frankincense, and proclaiming the praises of the Lord.

A reading from the Letter of Saint Paul to the Ephesians:

Brothers and sisters: You have heard of the stewardship of God's grace that was given to me for your benefit, namely, that the mystery was made known to me by revelation. It was not made known to people in other generations as it has now been revealed to his holy apostles and prophets by the Spirit: that the gentiles are coheirs, members of the same body, and copartners in the promise in Christ Jesus through the gospel.

A reading from the holy Gospel according to Matthew:

When Jesus was born in Bethlehem of Judea, in the days of King Herod, behold, magi from the east arrived in Jerusalem, saying, "Where is the newborn king of the Jews? We saw his star at its rising and have come to do him homage." When King Herod heard this, he was greatly troubled, and all Jerusalem with him. Assembling all the chief priests and the scribes of the people, he inquired of them where the Christ was to be born. They said to him, "In Bethlehem of Judea, for thus it has been written through the prophet: "And you, Bethlehem, land of Judea, are by no means least among the rulers of Judah; since from you shall come a ruler, who is to shepherd my people Israel." Then Herod called the magi secretly and ascertained from the time of the star's appearance. He sent them to Bethlehem and said, "Go and search diligently for the child. When you have found him, bring me word, that I to may go and do him homage." After their audience with the king they set out. And behold, the star that they had seen at its rising preceded them, until it came and stopped over the place where the child was. They were overjoyed at seeing the star, and on entering the house they saw the child with Mary his mother. They prostrated themselves and did him homage. Then they opened their treasures and offered him gifts of gold, frankincense, and myrrh. And having been warned in a dream not to return to Herod, they departed for their country by another way.

I could not see a thing. It was absolutely dark. So dark, in fact, that even when I held my hands in front of my eyes I could not see them. And I began to think that if I needed to find my way out of this predicament I would surely die, because I did not know the way out and I could not see.

I was in the second most famous prehistoric cave in south-central France called Rouffignac. If you have heard of the prehistoric cave systems in France, you have probably heard of Lascaux, which was discovered much earlier. But I was in Rouffignac and the guide, who had taken a group of us into the cave to see its prehistoric etchings, had decided, for reasons that I do not now remember, to turn out the light while we were in the belly of the cave. It was a very striking lesson to me, for now I know from that practical experience that one cannot have both light and darkness. They are mutually exclusive entities. There can be instances in the dark where very low levels of light can be found, but light exists nonetheless. One cannot have an instance of both light and absolute darkness.

Light is a very powerful symbol. It means so many things for us. It can refer to understanding. "Oh, I see the light!"

Light is a powerful image. It means things other than "we see", but even when we see it, it speaks to us. We see a flame burning in a candle, we see light. We see fire that gives off warmth and heat and light. We are fascinated by light. Personally-speaking, light reminds me of the third time I went through psychological testing.

I have had three instances of psychological testing in my life. The first time was when I attended seminary college. The second time was when I entered the seminary of the diocese. The third time was when I became a Dominican. I am an expert... anything you would like to know about psychological testing I can tell you. I have had them all. One test that must be taken is the Minnesota Multi-Phasic Personality Inventory. I have taken it three times. It is a commonly administered exam.

The Minnesota Multi-Phasic Personality Inventory, known as the MMPI, has a number of questions- 750 questions, I think, or something like that. The questions are actually statements, and one must either agree or disagree with them. Those are the only choices offered. The questions do not permit nuances and it is not possible to respond by saying, "Well, I do not know what this means."

I remember responding to one of the many MMPI ambiguous statements by filling in the little answer bubble, and that made me a little nervous, because I thought, "Well, if I respond truthfully to this statement my answer, taken out of context, might get me into some trouble."

The statement to which I was meant to respond was: "I am fascinated by fire."

Well... I am fascinated by fire. So... at first I thought that I should agree with the statement. But then I thought, "Well who knows what my agreeing to that statement will say about my state of mind."

When you are undergoing psychological testing you know that the examiners are looking for significant anomalies in the examinees. So, I thought, " If I say that I am fascinated by fire, God alone knows what the examiners are going to think of me. Will they think I am looking to torch a building or something like that?"

Yet, I could not escape from an honest response, because fire is fascinating. There is something about fire that captures our attention. Fire is a powerful image. Fire is a powerful symbol.

Today's readings speak much about light. They point out the mutual exclusivity of light and darkness. Read again the words spoken by the prophet Isaiah. *"Darkness covers the earth, and thick clouds cover the peoples..."*

These days we live in a world where we do not need to look very far to see darkness or thick clouds. In the not-too-distant past, we have seen devastating images of Asian shores, of our shores, and of the streets in the Middle East- parts of the world devastated by a horrific tsunami; parts of the world devastated by a hurricane named Katrina; innocent lives lost and whole families torn asunder by the relentless violence on the streets of Baghdad. Yes... *darkness covers the earth...*

When we look at our world, it becomes readily apparent that we live in an age of war and violence. Daily, we hear reports of people being killed somewhere... largely in the Middle East, but other places as well. *Thick clouds cover the peoples...*

I suspect we do not have to look too far from our own communities to know this to be true. I know many families in the northeast who have had to say goodbye to fathers and mothers, husbands and wives, brothers and sisters, because the soldiers among us have been deployed to Iraq. There are others among us who have personal struggles in their lives. Those who have dealt with illness or suffering. People see darkness because they may have discovered they have some terminal illness. There are those who have had to say good bye to loved ones, because their loved ones have died this year. Relationships can cause people pain and heartache, as well; husbands and wives, parents and children. It can be a time of real darkness and, indeed, other things we do not even need to mention, but things that can be part of the deep, dark suffering that is human existence, at times. And, were we to stop at those two little phrases, *"See, darkness covers the earth, and thick clouds cover the peoples..."* we might, indeed, give into despair and ask, "What is the point?"

Like one religious individual, who lives in Southeast Asia, the region affected by a massive tsunami, recently asked, (I do not know if he was a Christian, a Buddhist, or a Muslim), "Looking at all of this destruction, how can you speak of the love of God?"

There is some truth in such a question. And, were we to stop at those two little phrases, *"See, darkness covers the earth, and thick clouds cover the peoples..."* we might give into despair. Fortunately, Isaiah does not end his sentence where I stopped instead he said, *"See, darkness covers the earth, and thick clouds cover the peoples, **but**..."*

"But" is a very important word in that sentence, because it keeps us as people of hope even amid the darkness *"...but upon you the Lord shines, and over you appears his glory."*

You see... being a Christian has a lot to do with the light and how we see the world in which we live. It has to do with our vision, because Christ is of the light.

Jesus Christ is the light of the world, and upon you, and upon me, and upon us the glory of the Lord shines. We are people of the incarnation. We are people who have the experience of the manifestation of God as man.

It would have been easy in justice for God to say to all of humanity, (a mere two-thousand years ago), "Too bad... you sinned. Too bad for you... you are greedy. You are selfish. You do not love one another. You are hateful. You sin. You commit evil. You turn your back on me. Even though I show you a wonderful, life-giving way of light, you do not follow it. You do your own thing. You go astray. I am tired of it. I am not going to put up with it anymore."

But God did not say any of that. What God said was, "I am going to show them the best way I know how... how much I love them."

And *...by the power of the Holy Spirit he was born of the Virgin Mary, and became man...*

One of the many unbelievable aspects of this paradox is that, faced with the terrible scandal of sin, our God of justice, our God of mercy worked out an unbelievable deal for all of humanity. When Jesus died on the cross, Jesus got justice... We got the mercy. That is what the feast of the Epiphany is all about.

Let us take a look at the magi. They are odd characters. We do not know much about them except that they are described as coming from some vague area known as the East. People believe that they were astrologers, hence their interest in the stars. They had some indication that there was a newborn king of the Jews, but there is no indication that they understood what that meant. There is no indication that they were men of faith, or that they were even Jewish. We know so very little about them, but we do know that they knew how to read the signs of their age. They could follow stars.

Stars are interesting things. With the exception of one star we do not see stars during the daytime. We see only one star during the daytime and it is called the sun. We do not even think of the sun as being a star. We just think of it as being the sun. To see the other stars in the sky we have to wait until it is night. Occasionally, we see stars at the transition time; when it is not quite night, but still not quite day- dawn and dusk. Occasionally, what we think are stars are actually planets. The planet Venus comes to mind. We refer to Venus as the morning star and the evening star even though it is a planet. But Venus reflects light. It does not create it.

And so it is interesting that the magi were guided by a star in the darkness. There was light in the darkness. It helped them to see their way. But they became lost and unlike most men usually do, when the magi became lost they stopped to ask for directions. They did not ask the best fellow in the world, King Herod, but they did get the information they needed, and the information did get them back on the right track. They followed the star to Jesus.

When we look at what was going on in the world at that time, it was a world where the words of Isaiah were equally true. *"Darkness covers the earth, and thick clouds cover the peoples..."*

Herod was a cruel ruler. There was nothing nice about that fellow. Herod was a despot and that was why he was so concerned about any possible threat of a new king. We know what Herod did after his encounter with the magi... when he was tricked by the magi... when the magi did not return to him. King Herod ordered the death of every male child under the age of two. Herod was not a nice guy. *"Darkness covers the earth..."*

But, in the midst of this darkness was the Light of the World. And that, it seems to me, is the challenge of the Epiphany of the Lord.

The word Epiphany means manifestation. Jesus became known to the world, not simply to the Jews or to the people who knew the promise or the people who had been given the promise. Jesus was the great manifestation of the world. God, made man, now visible to everyone who was willing to see the sign.

Indeed, the second Vatican Counsil challenged the Church to do the very same thing: to read the sign of the times and to respond with the light of the Gospel, to consider the signs that were seen. And so today, it is not so much an historical feast where we look upon the event and say, "It was so nice of those magi to go and bestow such wonderful gifts upon Mary when Jesus was born."

I am sure Mary and Joseph could have used what money they received. I am sure Mary and Joseph were appreciative of the gifts they received. But that is not what the Epiphany of the Lord was about, then. That is not what the Epiphany of the Lord is about for us, today. The Epiphany of the Lord is a reflection on us as a people of hope, because we are people of the light of Christ.

How do we combat a world that seems so overwhelmingly overcome by evil?

By gathering together, together in the fellowship of worship and spiritual celebration.

By coming together in the fellowship of worship and spiritual celebration we see the light of Christ becoming present on the altar.

By receiving the light of Christ, by receiving Jesus in the Eucharist, by coming together week in and week out, and in many instances, day after day to celebrate the Eucharist.

And by doing so, we will be able to see clearly. We will be able to see as God sees. We will become people of wisdom.

That is precisely how you can look at people who deal with suffering and see in those who suffer some who despair and others who have hope. It has everything to do with the way they see. Those who hope see meaning and purpose and presence in the world. That is why it is so important for us to gather together each week, because God helps us to see clearly.

God gives us the light. God helps us to understand our world. God helps us to understand the way things are.

Ours is not a case where we need to do all kinds of things to make God present in the world, but certainly our love for God will let the world know that God is present. The first step... our primary step... the most important step... is always to recognize that God is God. We cannot always make sense of things, but we can always depend upon our relationship with God.

And so, on this great feast of the Epiphany of the Lord... the manifestation of our God... God's presence in our world... let us pray that we might heed the message Isaiah sends to us, from an age long gone by, so that nations will walk by our light, kings by our shining radiance, and all may come to see us, radiant and in our radiance. We are indeed radiant, because of the life giving light of our Lord Jesus Christ.

Fr. De Porres

We believe in one Lord, Jesus Christ, the only Son of God, eternally begotten of the Father, God from God, Light from Light, true God from true God, begotten, not made, one in being with the Father...

Baptism of the Lord

A reading from the Book of the Prophet Isaiah:

Thus says the Lord: "Here is my servant whom I uphold, my chosen one with whom I am pleased, upon whom I have put my spirit, he shall bring forth justice to the nations, not crying out, not shouting, not making his voice heard in the street. A bruised reed he shall not break, and a smoldering wick he shall not quench, until he establishes justice on the earth; the coastlines will wait for his teaching. I, the Lord, have called you for the victory of justice, I have grasped you by the hand; I formed you, and set you as a covenant of the people, a light for the nations, to open the eyes of the blind, to bring out prisoners from confinement, and from the dungeon, those who live in darkness."

A reading from the Acts of the Apostles:

Peter proceeded to speak to those gathered in the house of Cornelius, saying: "In truth, I see that God shows no partiality. Rather, in every nation whoever fears him and acts uprightly is acceptable to him. You know the word that he sent to the Israelites as he proclaimed peace through Jesus Christ, who is Lord of all, what has happened all over Judea, beginning in Galilee after the baptism that John preached, how God anointed Jesus of Nazareth with the holy spirit and power. He went about doing good and healing all those oppressed by the devil, for God was with him."

A reading from the holy Gospel according to Matthew:

Jesus came from Galilee to John at the Jordan to be baptized by him. John tried to prevent him, saying, "I need to be baptized by you, and yet you are coming to me?" Jesus said to him in reply, "Allow it now, for thus it is fitting for us to fulfill all righteousness." Then he allowed him. After Jesus was baptized, he came up from the water and behold, the heavens were opened for him, and he saw the spirit of God descending like a dove and coming upon him. And a voice came from the heavens, saying, "This is my beloved Son, with whom I am well pleased."

And so my brothers and sisters are you saved?

Have you found Jesus in your life?

Have you accepted Jesus as your Lord and Savior?

If this were a different type of congregation you would hear questions similar to those all of the time, because they are important questions in certain circles of Christianity. And on some level, I suspect, this question of salvation is important for us as well, because deep down that is what we all want to know.

Are we going to be saved?

What do we need to do for salvation?

The feast of the Baptism of the Lord gives us the occasion to think about what is meant by salvation, and how salvation is received.

I would suggest to you that there are three aspects of salvation we need to think about. First of all, there is the question concerning the baptism of Jesus, itself. The baptism of Jesus was problematic for the early Church. It took some time for the Church to figure out what the baptism of Jesus meant. Secondly, there is the question concerning the baptism of us, as Catholics. What does our baptism mean? What do we believe about our baptism? Lastly, there is the question concerning what salvation means for those who are not Catholic or those who are not Christians. What does the Church teach about salvation for non-Christians or other types of Christians?

The baptism of Jesus was a problem for the early Church, and we get an inkling of that fundamental problem in the Gospel of Saint John. The baptism of Jesus was a problem for the early Church, because there was conflict within the early Church between those who believed that John the Baptist was the Messiah and those who believed the Messiah was yet to come. The early Church was conflicted in this matter, because John the Baptist was doing Messiah-like things: he was preaching repentance; he was baptizing. All of these things were occurring in the Jordan. John the Baptist had disciples. We know this from other sections of the Gospel where John the Baptist even sent his disciples to ask Jesus a question about whether or not Jesus was the Messiah. But the Gospel of Saint John goes to great lengths to say that while John the Baptist was very special, indeed, even Jesus said, *"... among those born of woman there has arisen no one greater than John the Baptist..."* John the Baptist was not the Messiah.

As he is quoted in the Gospel, Saint John makes it clearly known that John the Baptist was not the Messiah. So why was it that Jesus felt the need or was called to be baptized by him?

Why?

We believe today that Jesus is the sacramental giver of baptism. We are able to be baptized because of Jesus. The second person of the blessed Trinity, the Son of God, cannot be in need of baptism in the way we are. The answer to the question previously posed is found, I believe, in the line at the end of today's Gospel reading. *"This is my beloved Son, with whom I am well pleased."*

The baptism of Jesus was a revelatory experience. And while the lines of the Gospels according to Matthew, Mark, Luke, and John are a bit different... depending on who's telling the story... the basic message is the same: when Jesus was baptized, something miraculous occurred, and people heard it. It was not just an interior experience for our Lord. There was something in the baptism of Jesus that everyone experienced. Namely, they heard the voice of God tell people who that person, Jesus, was.

In today's Gospel reading, God told the people, *"This is my beloved Son, with whom I am well pleased."*

In another Gospel reading, God is quoted as saying, *"This is my beloved son in whom I am well pleased. Listen to him."*

Much like the Epiphany, with the manifesting moment that Jesus was not an ordinary human being, the baptism of Jesus was a revelatory experience; an experience of God, where God leaves no doubt that Jesus is not simply a nice guy who went around doing good things, but that He is the second person of the blessed Trinity. He is the Son of God. He is the Divine God, who became man. And so, the baptism of Jesus says something about who Jesus is. This is a very important point because all of the blessed sacraments rest upon who Jesus is.

If Jesus was just a nice guy... then, we should not be teaching the Sacraments as the Church understands them. We should be teaching something else: symbolic meals, nice actions, things that remind us of what God might do. Yet, today, we teach about the sacramental system we believe as Catholics, where we encounter Christ in every Sacrament. Hence, the baptism of Jesus.

What about our own baptism?

During my celebration of mass on New Year's Day, I spoke of a heresy I believe most of us share. At the very least, deep down inside of ourselves we fight against it and the Church has fought against it from the beginning as well. It is one of the very first heresies the Church condemned. It was the Church's reaction to the teachings of a fellow named Pelagius, who simply believed this: our good works earned salvation for us. To put it in a simpler context, at the end of our life, God will take His scale out, and on one side He will place our good works and on the other side He will place our evil deeds, and which ever weighs more will determine whether or not we are saved.

Very early on, the Church recognized that such a belief in salvation, as espoused by Pelagius, was absolutely, utterly, and entirely wrong. Essentially, that is what heresy means: it is wrong. Speaking on salvation, the Church said, "At the very heart of salvation lies the premise that no one deserves salvation."

One cannot earn salvation, because nobody deserves salvation. If God gave us what we deserve, we would be condemned, because **we sin**.

No one can say, "I have a right to salvation!"

No one can say, "I have earned salvation. See... I have done all of these good deeds."

No one can say such things. Salvation is a free gift. None of us deserve it. God gives salvation to us for one reason and one reason alone: God loves us!

Now, that does not mean we can do whatever we please without consequence, but it does mean that we cannot earn salvation. Salvation is a free gift. God gives it to us.

God gives it to us for God loves us.

In the beginning everything was wonderful. At the very beginning of creation we had a paradise. We had everything we could want. The world was not in conflict or competition. Man was not pitted against man. Man was not pitted against woman. Man was not pitted against animal, nor against his environment. Everything was in perfect balance, in perfect harmony. There was but one rule we had to follow. There was only one thing we had to worry about.

"You shall not eat of the fruit of the tree that is in the midst of the garden, the tree of knowledge of good and evil."

That is how we get into trouble... is it not? If we simply accepted the fact that certain things are wrong and certain things are right, God would be satisfied with us and we would not have to worry about life.

The only rule we had to worry about was: *"You shall not eat of the fruit of the tree..."*

But the problem was this... it was not the eating of the fruit... it was: I do not like the rule.

The tree looks good. The fruit looks good. I'll bet the fruit tastes good.

It is written in Scripture that *"The tree was good for food and that it was a delight to the eyes and that the tree was desired to make one wise."*

"But I do not like the rule."

"I want to make the rule."

That is what sin is...!

"I want to make the rules. I do not like God's rules. I want to make my own rules. I do not want to be kind to others. I want to be selfish. I want things my way. I do not want to think of any one else. I want to think of me. I do not want to share what I have. I want to be greedy. I want to horde things for myself. I do not like God's rules."

You see... therein lays the problem.

And where did we get that? We got that from the very beginning, because we decided that we did not like God's rule. And it skewed us.

Our will became defective. Things that appeared not to be of God looked attractive to us. We chose those things against the will of God.

At that moment, God could have said of us, "Well, too bad for you. There is no hope for you. I gave you one simple rule and you could not even follow that."

But God loves us. And so God said, "Nope. I am going to give you another chance, but I am going to give you that chance in a dramatic way. I am going to send my son, who is going to die so that your sins will be forgiven."

God took the justice upon Himself.

Who got what we deserve?

God did.

Jesus did.

Jesus died for our sins. We got the mercy. We got the benefits. Easy enough... right? Makes perfect sense... right?

We need to keep in mind that salvation is a free gift. That is why the Catholic Church and the early Church fathers underscored it with passion. That is why Catholics do not have any difficulty baptizing infants.

There is concern among certain Christian denominations that when infants are baptized they are unable to accept baptism. Catholics do not see this conflict or contradiction in the baptizing of infants, because salvation is a free gift.

Salvation is a **free** gift. You do not have to do anything to be saved. You just have to accept God's salvation. Ultimately, at some point in our tradition, people do accept God's salvation. But the gift of baptism helps our will. Things that appear to be from God, appear more like they are from God... so we are more likely to choose those things despite our defective wills, wills that are defective because of sin. That is what our own baptism means.

There are, of course, obligations that go along with such matters, and I will address them in a minute. If we are really serious about accepting salvation, (again, such does not mean we can do whatever we please), there are things we must do. There is a way of living our lives that is part and parcel to accepting God's salvation. Accepting God's salvation means certain things.

What about people who are not Christians?

There are theologians who suggest that the most difficult aspect of faith for Americans is that Americans have a notion of equality. This notion of equality is fundamental to our acceptance of democracy. And equality is a good thing. I am not here to speak against equality, per se. Equal rights is a good thing. Everyone deserves the same human rights. But some theologians suggest equality is a problem for American Christians, because we have a temptation to think that every idea is equal, or that every choice is of equal merit; or that everyone's opinion is of equal value, or that everyone's personal choices are of equal value.

Some theologians suggest that such thinking lays at the heart of the problem with American Christian philosophy, because when we begin to talk about some things being better or worse than others, about some choices being better or worse than others, we bristle. Some of us will not even accept such a premise. Yet, we know that not everything can be equally good. There is such a thing as sin. There are such things as bad choices. All we need to do is to look at the television and realize that some people make bad choices. Some people make bad decisions. Some people sin. There is evil in our world. We can look at ourselves and we can say, "I sin."

Not everything to which we subscribe is good or is good all the time.

In a similar vein, we have a tendency to believe that a certain equality exists between all who believe in Jesus Christ. We have a tendency to believe that every Christian religion is as good as another. We have been led to believe that, and we subscribe to that way of thinking. Well... that is just plain nonsense, especially if we take the time to think such things through. This is where it gets difficult for us.

There has to be, on some level, (if we really believe what we say we believe), something qualitatively different about being a Catholic than being another type of Christian. There has to be. Otherwise it would not matter that we assemble in our church, in the fellowship of our faith. We could be anywhere on Sunday. We could be in any church and it would be just as good. And the problem is this... if the latter is true, then why would God reveal anything? Why would we need the Gospels? Why would we need the Scriptures? If everything is equally as true, why would we need any of those things that are so important to our faith?

Now, another problem arises here as well. Because of this difference, the difference between being a Catholic and being a Christian of another denomination, such a subscription can be easily misused. And it has been misused.

Recall the first of our readings this day. God wants to save everyone. God shows no partiality. Salvation is open to every man, woman, and child that God created, because God loves everybody... and He can love everyone.

Historically, there was a quote from the Pope that was misused: "Outside the Church there is no salvation."

If the entire papal document was read, the reader would come to know that the Pope's intention was to show that the Church is broad and inclusive. In other words, the net cast by the Church gathers in a multitude of souls. Unfortunately, that is not the interpretation by which the quote is usually construed. The Holy Father's words have been misused as a result.

What does the Church teach about salvation and other Christians, or salvation and non-Christians?

The second Vatican counsel was very clear: "The Church is the best way to salvation. The Church is the easiest way to salvation, because we believe the Church was founded, is guided, and is graced by Jesus Christ. Jesus set up the Church; God gives the Church grace. So in its significant areas of teaching, the Church is graced by the Holy Spirit."

Now, that is not to say that every decision is directly guided by the Holy Spirit, but it speaks to the fact that our traditions, our fundamental doctrines, and our dogmas are. Our belief that Jesus Christ is truly present in the Holy Eucharist is just one example of this. The Church said, "The easiest way to salvation is through the Church, by being a Catholic."

On some level, I think that if you are a Catholic you are inclined to subscribe to the latter sentiment. But the Church did not say one could not be saved by following different paths.

Salvation always comes through Jesus. And that makes sense. Jesus told us, *"I am the way, the truth, and the light."*

Not always explicit, but always important, Jesus is the method of salvation. Here, however, is what the Church said, "It is possible to obtain God's salvation as a member of another church, insofar as it contains truth."

It is possible to find God's salvation as a Buddhist, insofar as there are truths in that religion.

Now, that brings it back to us. There is a lot of attention given to our diocese, and others as well, given the fact that the number of priests is declining. Even in dioceses that are doing well by their vocations, every priest who dies or retires cannot be replaced. What has not been given as much attention is the fact that in areas like the Northeast the number of Catholics has declined almost at the same rate. You do not hear much about that or the fact that we find similar ratios of Catholics to priests. In other parts of our country such is not true. There are parts of the West and of the Southwest, where the number of Mexican-American Catholics is overwhelming. Their numbers are growing by leaps and bounds, and the number of Catholics is easily outpacing the number of priests, but not in the Northeast. And that brings us back to the first reading.

When we say we accept God's salvation, we believe we can live forever by simply accepting what Jesus wants to give us. That means we must live our lives in a particular way. But if we really believe that this is a fundamentally, life-changing thing... that eternal life is open to us... that this is better than we could possibly deserve and is certainly more powerful and life giving than we could possibly imagine... then why would we choose to keep that knowledge to ourselves? That is the challenge facing Catholics.

I admire the Mormons or the Jehovah Witnesses for this reason: They go out!

Mormons have to. You cannot be a Mormon and not mission. For two years, members of the Mormon faith go out to where they are sent by their elders. They can be sent anywhere, and they go. They go and they talk about their faith. They want others to know about it. There is something about their faith they want everyone to be aware. Well, that is part of what it means to accept salvation.

Saint Thomas Aquinas talked about sharing faith in these terms. If I have a piece of pie and I say I want to share it with you... if you accept my offer... then I have less pie. Some things that are good reduce when they are shared. If I possess a certain amount of money and I share it with you, or I give it to charity... I end up with less money. But the best things, said Saint Thomas Aquinas, do not reduce when they are shared... just the opposite occurs. The best things are every bit as plentiful despite the fact that they have been shared.

Love is an example of such a thesis.

When you love someone you do not have less love for everyone else. In the sharing of your love, you actually end up with more love.

The same thing is true of God's love. When God loves us, it is not as though through God's love for a billion people His love for us is reduced by half when another billion people come along. Saint Thomas Aquinas observed that love grows when it is shared. That is just the way it works. And there are other things like that. Salvation works in that way. When we accept our salvation we will experience the comfort and the solace of our salvation in greater measure when we share our knowledge of it... when we talk about it. Great things will happen to us, and for us, when we are willing to share what we believe and how such beliefs make a difference in our lives.

Catholics are not as good about sharing their faith as they should be. We do not like to talk about our faith. Such an observation is a little less true of Catholics who live in the mid-West.   In New England, Catholics do not like to talk about personal things like faith. Catholics in the mid-West do; they are much more willing to share their faith and to talk about it.

Such was my experience when I lived in Colorado. Catholic children in Colorado wear their faith on their sleeve... so to speak. Now, it is not like no one in New England talks about their faith...that is not entirely true, because many of us do. But today's feast of the Baptism of the Lord is a challenge to each of us to share the great gift that God has given us. The gift of Salvation. And if we do... just imagine how wonderful it will be when God says to us... to each one of us... you are my beloved son, you are my beloved daughter *...with whom I am well pleased.*

Fr. De Porres

Through Him all things were made...

Second Sunday in Ordinary Time

A reading from the Book of the Prophet Isaiah:

The Lord said to me: "You are my servant, Israel, through whom I show my glory. Now the Lord has spoken who formed me as his servant from the womb, that Jacob may be brought back to him and Israel gathered to him; and I am made glorious in the sight of the Lord, and my God is now my strength! It is too little, the Lord says, for you to be my servant, to raise up the tribes of Jacob, and restore the survivors of Israel; I will make you a light to the nations, that my salvation may reach to the ends of the earth."

A reading from the first Letter of Saint Paul to the Corinthians:

Paul, called to be an apostle of Christ Jesus by the will of God, and Sosthenes our brother, to the church of God that is in Corinth, to you who have been sanctified in Christ Jesus, called to be holy, with all those everywhere who call upon the name of our Lord Jesus Christ, their Lord and ours. Grace to you and peace from God our Father and the Lord Jesus Christ.

A reading from the holy Gospel according to John:

John the Baptist saw Jesus coming toward him and said, "Behold, the Lamb of God, who takes away the sin of the world. He is the one of whom I said, 'A man is coming after me who ranks ahead of me because he existed before me.' I did not know him, but the reason why I came baptizing with water was that he might be made known to Israel." John testified further, saying, "I saw the Spirit come down like a dove from heaven and remain upon him. I did not know him, but the one who sent me to baptize with water told me, 'On whomever you see the Spirit come down and remain, he is the one who will baptize with the Holy Spirit.' Now I have seen and testified that he is the Son of God."

Catholic Mass is always begun with the Penitential Rite. Then, after we have asked God to forgive us our sins and to help us live the Gospel, we have an opening prayer. In the opening prayer we ask God for something. Each Sunday we petition God for something. It may be similar to the previous Sunday, but our petitions are never the same.

This morning I asked God for two things. On your behalf, and mine, I asked for God to hear our prayer and that we may find a way to bring peace to the world. I did not ask this of the Lord in my name or yours... I asked it in the name of Jesus Christ, *"Your Son, our Lord, who lives and reigns with You in unity with the Holy Spirit, one God forever and ever."*

And you must have liked the opening prayer, because you said, "Amen."

So, let it be that way. It is what we want... for God to hear our prayers and for us to find a way to bring peace to the world.

How does God answer us?

God answers us with through our readings of Scripture. And that is what today's Scripture readings are about. All of today's readings are almost identical. Today's Scripture readings are about who we are and who God is.

Sometimes we lose track of who we are and of who God is. When the roles of parents and children are reversed, we fall into trouble. When the roles of teachers and students are reversed, we fall into trouble. When spouses or priest or religious leaders forget who they are... we are in trouble.

When we know who we are... and accept who we are... and rejoice in who we are... things are fine.

The responsorial Psalm sung for us today by the Saint Francis Xavier Choir is entitled *Here I am Lord, I come to do Your Will*.

"Here I am Lord, I come to do your will."

That is a mouthful, is it not?

"... I come to do your will."

Have you ever put the cart before the horse?

Think about that question for a minute.

Have you ever had a time in your life when you had a heavy cross to bear?

Did you ever have a time in your life when things were not going your way?

Well, of course you have. Who has not... that is life. We have all experienced such emotions at one time or another.

Was there ever a time in your life when you felt that things were all topsy-turvy... and when you felt that way, did you get down on your knees to pray to God?

In your prayers to God, did you ask God to do it your way?

"God, would you see things through my eyes... through my lenses!?"

"God, would you turn it around? I do not like things the way they are!"

"Would you come Lord... to do my will!?"

We have all felt that way, at one time or another, have we not?

And when God did not do things the way we wanted them done, do we find ourselves saying, *"That is not fair!"*

"That is not right!"

"What have I done to deserve this?"

Have you ever looked at things from the other side of the mirror?

Sometimes we blame God for not doing things the way we want them done. After all, we have said our prayers and still things have not turned out the way we thought or wished they should be.

On the other hand, when things are sailing along quite smoothly in our lives... when everything is just honky-dory... how many times have we **not** thanked God?

How many times have you thanked God for the breath you take... for the heartbeat in your chest... for the pulse in your veins... for the food in your stomach... for the air in your lungs... for the rain upon your flowers... for the sun upon your fields... for the roof above your head... for the bed under your back... for the pillow under your head... for the family gathered at your table... for the friend at the other end of the telephone line... and on and on and on...?

We take such things for granted, do we not?

We find it easier to beg than to praise, do we not?

We really think that our plan for reality is better than God's plan for our reality, do we not?

Let us look at Isaiah. Isaiah tells us who we are. And that is some-thing we too often forget.

We are many things... and many things we are not. However, Isaiah gave us something very specific to dwell upon in today's reading. He started out with this: *The Lord said to me, "You are my servant."*

Now bite on that one.

"You are my servant."

There are two people, whom I know, who did that very thing, very well. Two people who did not mind being called servants of God. One of those people is Jesus and the other is Jesus' mother, Mary. Mary even called herself the handmaid of the Lord. Jesus always said he was the servant of His Father.

One line from today's responsorial goes like this... it is very beautiful and it gives us our vocation. The line reads, *"As the eyes of the servant are on the hand of the master may our eyes be on you, oh Lord."*

What does that mean?

"As the eyes of the servant are on the hand of the master may our eyes be on you, oh Lord."

It is about a banquet... really! The master was at the head of the table, and the servants were lined up with food and wine and with any-thing the guests might need. The servants were very well trained... and they never took their eyes off the master.

Do you know what they waited for?

They waited for the summoning finger of their master.

They waited for their master to snap his fingers or to motion them with his index finger, bading them, "Come."

The immediate response of the servant is what is important. Do you mind being a servant of the Lord?

How do we become a servant of the Lord?

Isaiah did not leave it there... once we come to grips with being a servant of the Lord... he gave us more: *"It is too little," the Lord says, "for you to be my servant." "I will make you a light to the nations."*

A servant who is a light.

A servant with a lamp.

Would like to understand that a little bit more... to know what your vocation is?

Tonight, get yourself a little pocket flashlight and go down into your cellar. Once you are down there... turn off all of the lights. Go to the furthest recess of the cellar. Now... try to find your way out of your cellar without bumping into something, without hurting yourself, without falling on the stairs.

Having tried that... now take out your penlight and turn it on. You are safe. You can find the way out.

You must be a light to the nations- the servant with the flashlight; the servant who shows the way.

In order to do all of that, there are certain qualities we must possess... and we find them in our Lady, who never minded being a servant of God; and in Jesus, who even called himself the servant of God. One has to start with the emptying of self. We see that in John the Baptist. It is not about John the Baptist. It is about Jesus. It is not about us. To see God's will... you have to let go of your will.

A shaker cannot contain salt and pepper at the same time. If it does... you end up with neither salt nor pepper.

"I come to do your will."

We need humility to know who God is... and to know who we are. We need humility to be able to say we are the handmaid... we are the servant of the Lord. We find such humility through the holiness of spirit.

Therese of Lisieux was fond of saying that she was the Lord's broom... and when God was finished with her, He put her behind the door until He needed her again... and that was all right with her. That is why the "little flower" became a great saint. She let God use her. Every breath of her body was for God. She knew the vocation of Carmel. The vocation of Carmel was to be the garden, the garden set apart in the Church... for the Church... and for others.

With humility comes littleness; a little light that leads to the big light. Never take the flashlight and put in on your own face. Put it on Christ. It goes on Christ. It belongs on Christ. In that way, when we return home we will no longer need the flashlight. Jesus Christ is the light.

In humility... in joy... in great love... not in manipulation, but in service... there is a difference. Manipulation seeks **my** will. Service seeks **the** will of the other.

Saint Paul tells us a bit more about who we are and about who God is.

The entire reading we have this day from Saint Paul to the Corinthians is nothing but a greeting. It is not even the heart of the matter, it is: *"I, Paul, am an apostle of Jesus Christ."*

Saint Paul knew what the flashlight meant. John the Baptist knew what the flashlight meant. Can you not see that nothing has changed. Would you have liked to have been there when the Lamb of God was pointed out?

You are.

What is the difference between being in the Jordan and hearing John the Baptist say, *"Behold, the Lamb of God"* and your priest holding up the Holy Eucharist and saying, "Behold, the Lamb of God"?

Faith is easier for us nowadays, because we have the faith of baptism. In the days of John the Baptist and Saint Paul, people had to accept something without the faintest notion or idea as to what it was about. We are the denizens.

The next thing to being a servant of God is to look under our noses. How do we serve?

Well, the answer is right there. You do not have to move. You do not have to go anywhere. You will know how to serve.   The answer is right there with you. The answer is: Use the talents that God has given to you.

I know many wonderful people... but right now I will recall for you the memory of one particularly wonderful person. This one person has always impressed me, greatly. In her I have always found such great love and such great ability to grasp what is called the sacrament of the present moment. The person of whom I am thinking is possessive of a marvelous talent, she is a financial genius. She has a mind like a computer and an adding machine. Numbers on ledgers in books... she is a wiz at such things.

Several years ago this person was engaged in bookkeeping, in reconciling the finances of not only the parish of Saint Francis Xavier, but other entities as well. One day she decided she wanted to return to the spirit of her founders. So, she devised a plan to retreat from all of her entanglements. She said that she really wanted to serve the poor "one on one."

"I want to go back. I want to be of service to the real poor," she said to me.

She went to one of our patron charities, one that takes care of the poor. She presented herself there and introduced herself by saying, "I will give you two or three days a week. I need to serve the poor. I am not a bad cook. I am not opposed to washing or drying dishes. I do not mind mopping floors or doing windows.   I do not mind changing beds or doing the laundry, and I do not mind sitting down with people and talking with them. So, whatever you would like me to do... here I am."

"I come to do your will."

And the sister who was in charge of this particular charity looked at her and said, "Oh sister, thank-you so much. I know who you are. Sister... our books are such a mess!"

She went home with a new set of books to balance...

It was not the way she wanted it... but God love her... she did what was needed of her, and she used what she knew.

The answer is there. It is inside of each of us. We all have value... and the vocation of John the Baptist is not much different than your vocation or mine. Collectively, as a church, and individually, we have the same mission: Be the light... the light that is not shined upon us, but the one that we shine upon others. And with hearts filled with joy it is our mission to say, " Behold! The Lamb of God!"

"I am only one... but I am one. I cannot do everything... but I can do something. What I can do... I ought to do. And what I ought to do... by the grace of God, I will do."

Those beautiful words were spoken by Sister Mary Peter Moore.

Fr. Lavalley

For us and for our salvation He came down from heaven: by the power of the Holy Spirit He was born of the Virgin Mary, and became man...

Third Sunday in Ordinary Time

A reading from the Book of the Prophet Isaiah:

First the Lord degraded the land of Zebulun and the land of Naphtali; but in the end he has glorified the seaward road, the land west of the Jordan, the District of the Gentiles.

Anguish has taken wing, dispelled is darkness: for there is no gloom where but now there was distress. The people who walked in darkness have seen a great light; upon those who dwelt in the land of gloom a light has shone. You have brought them abundant joy and great rejoicing, as they rejoice before you at the harvest, as people make merry when dividing spoils. For the yoke that burdened them, the pole on their shoulder, and the rod of their taskmaster you have smashed, as on the day of Midian.

A reading from the first Letter of Saint Paul to the Corinthians:

I urge you, brothers and sisters, in the name of our Lord Jesus Christ, that all of you agree in what you say, and that there be no divisions among you, but that you be united in the same mind and in the same purpose. For it has been reported to me about you, my brothers and sisters, by Chloe's people, that there are rivalries among you. I mean that each of you is saying, "I belong to Paul," or "I belong to Apollos," or "I belong to Cephas," or "I belong to Christ." Is Christ divided? Was Paul crucified for you? Or were you baptized in the name of Paul? For Christ did not send me to baptize but to preach the gospel, and not with the wisdom of human eloquence, so that the cross of Christ might not be emptied of its meaning.

A reading from the holy Gospel according to Matthew:

When Jesus heard that John had been arrested, he withdrew to Galilee. He left Nazareth and went to live in Capernaum by the sea, in the region of Zebulun and Naphtali, that what had been said through Isaiah the prophet might be fulfilled: "Land of Zebulun and land of Naphtali, the way to the sea, beyond the Jordan, Galilee of the Gentiles, the people who sit in darkness have seen a great light, on those dwelling in a land overshadowed by death light has arisen." From that time on, Jesus began to preach and say, "Repent, for the kingdom of heaven is at hand."

As he was walking by the sea of Galilee, he saw two brothers, Simon, who is called Peter, and his brother Andrew, casting a net into the sea; they were fishermen. He said to them, "Come after me, and I will make you fishers of men." At once they left their nets and followed him. He walked along from there and saw two other brothers, James, the son of Zebedee, and his brother John. They were in a boat, with their father Zebedee, mending their nets. He called them, and immediately they left their boat and their father and followed him.

He went around all of Galilee, teaching in their synagogues, proclaiming the gospel of the kingdom, and curing every disease and illness among the people.

There is so much more to us, individually and collectively, if we would just take a closer look at ourselves. Let us go outside mentally for a minute. Let us use this season and the weather. It is cold outside. The ground is frozen. Pipes are frozen, too. The snow is deep and it, too, has a cover of frost upon it. And, right now the snow makes an awful sound when you walk upon it. The sound goes right up through your shoes. You know the sound. Scrunch, scrunch... crinkle, crinkle. The sound travels up through your feet; up through your spine; right up to your head. The only sound out there is the sound of ice. It does not appear as though it will ever change, does it?

But, we know there will be a Spring, because underneath all of that frost and snow there is life. We do not see it, but we believe it. We know change is going to come, because God does the same thing with the seasons every year.

Just the other day a friend recited for me that old rhyme we were taught when we were children. You know the one:

"Thirty days hath September, April, June, and November. All the rest have thirty-one, save February which has twenty-eight clear, and January... which has a hundred and thirty."

It seems like that right now... does it not? Yet, we know what God will soon do. Soon He will send the warmth of the sun to shine upon us and there will be Spring... and grass... and the trees will have leaves... and warm breezes will blow. We will joyously discard our sweaters and our coats. We will open our windows and enjoy the fresh, warm air. And the birds will return to our trees.

We cannot see it, but it will happen, because there is life in that frozen ground.

Have you ever felt like what it is out there?

Have you ever felt cold?

Oh... I do not mean the body. Of course, we feel such cold on a day like today.... but I mean inside.

Have you ever felt cold?

Have you ever felt as though your heart was frozen to its core?

Have you ever felt so cold and so frigid inside that you thought you could never pray again?

Or love again?

Or forgive again?

Or reach out again?

Or give again?

Have you ever felt as though there could not possibly be any life in your heart?

Oh... there is life in there.

Today, in the opening prayer of mass we did not ask God for the gift of love. What we asked of God was for Him to direct the love that is within our hearts. I do not care how old your heart is today or how cold your heart is today, or anything else: God's love is within your heart. It was put there in baptism. I do not care how many sheets of ice cover that love... it is there. Just like the frozen ground right outside our door needs the sun, your love needs the same thing the world outside needs: the warmth of the sun. Except, the sun we need is spelled S-O-N.

The Son of God.

Just as the rays of the sun can melt all of that frozen nonsense outside, the rays of the Son can melt the coldest heart.

Saint Paul knew this.

Saint Paul was afraid of one thing and one thing only.

He was not afraid of being shipwrecked; been there, done that.

He was not afraid of scourging; been there, done that.

He was not afraid of imprisonment; been there, done that.

He was not afraid of imprisonment. He was not afraid of death. He was not afraid of anything that had to do with himself or the Church. He was not afraid of anything that could hurt himself or the Church from the outside... but the one thing Saint Paul was most afraid of was what could hurt himself or the Church from the inside. He was afraid of anything that could destroy God's love. For that reason, Saint Paul does not say, "Be careful of being caught. Be careful of being scourged. Be careful not to... (any one of a million things.)"

Saint Paul said, "Be careful not to gossip. Be careful not to quarrel. Be careful not to **not** speak to one another because of your theological position: Liberal or conservative. Scribe or Pharisee."

If you shun anyone, because you believe such a person is not of Christ, then you are not of Christ. And if I shun anyone because I believe such a person is not of Christ, then I am not of Christ.

Saint Paul was afraid of cancer. The kind of cancer that can corrode that which is found within the body: the Soul. That is why Saint Paul said, "It does not matter what road you travel upon to reach Christ. Are you a Carmelite? Are you a Dominican? Are you a Benedictine? Are you a Liberal? Are you a Conservative? Are you a Right? Are you a Left? Are you a this? Are you a that?"

"Are you of Christ?"

Of course we are different... Saint Paul said as much. Rhetorically, Saint Paul asked, "Do you think the eye does not know that it is not the ear?"

Saint Paul said, "I am not called to baptize. I am called to preach."

Know who you are.

Each one of us has a wonderful power within. How do I know it is there?

What can we do with it?

Let us take a look at the commandment of Jesus in the Gospel. The answer is there.

Jesus needed people.

I am going to say that again.

Jesus needed people.

And when he lost people... Jesus felt the loss.

Grace comes to us through others. Now, I am going to turn that around and challenge you with it. You are called to be a grace for others. And if we forget that... our concept of grace is to us what food is to a hamster.

I used to have a hamster when I was a child. Hamsters do not eat just enough food for one day. They store large amounts of food in their cheeks.

You are not called to be a spiritual hamster.

We need people... and people need us. And do not forget the first part of today's Gospel. Let us take a look at it.

John the Baptist was arrested.

Jesus and John had known one another for a long time. The first time John met Jesus, he was in the womb of his mother: Elizabeth. And when Jesus, while still within the womb of our Lady, came into the presence of Elizabeth, little Johnny started kicking. He was so happy to see Him. He was always happy to see Him. His cousin was his life.

A relationship is a two way street... and there came a time when Jesus said, *"Truly, I say to you, among those born of women there has arisen no one greater than John the Baptist."*

John was arrested... and he did not make it out of jail. He was beheaded. Jesus never saw John the Baptist, again... in this world. Oh... He saw him again, but not in this world.

Did you notice what Jesus did when He heard the news of the arrest of John the Baptist?

Did you miss it?

Do you see how easy it is to pass over such things?

Jesus moved out of Nazareth. He was just a hometown boy, but they were so hostile to Him. So, He moved. He went to Capernaum by the sea, which was not such a great move either.

Do you know why?

Land of Zebulun and land of Naphtali... it was pagan territory. The residents of Zebulun and Naphtali did not understand that Jewish boy, particularly the One who is divine.

Today's translation of this particular Gospel passage is so very polite. It never used to be that way. Today's translation of this Gospel calls it: *Galilee of the Gentiles.*

Do you know what the old translation called it?

Heathen Galilee... heathen Galilee... pagan country.

Galilee of the Gentiles... it is so very polite. A rose by any other name...

Jesus had a house there. A house that we will revisit in Scripture. A house that is going to lose its roof, because a paralytic falls through it. But in today's Gospel passage, Jesus was walking. Would you deny the fact that He was probably very lonely?

Do not rob Jesus of His humanity.

And do not rob yourself of yours. Humanity is a gift from God. All of it.

Jesus was walking and He saw a little speck on the beach.

It was not John... it was somebody else.

The one on the beach was kind of hard to take at times.

He was a great big burly fisherman, one who had a habit of thinking he knew much more than he really did. And, very often, that fisherman had a problem of speaking before he thought. He was impetuous. He thought he knew it all. In reality, and at this point in the Gospel, he did not really know anything... yet.

He thought that day was a day just like any other day. He was probably not much to look at... he was probably kind of dirty... he had been dealing with fish all day. (Fish in the day before Right Guard) His brother was there, as well. They were not much to look at... the pair of them... but Jesus saw something in them. He saw you... and He saw me.

Then... a most ridiculous thing happened. Jesus looked at the fishermen and said, *"Follow me, and I will make you fishers of men."*

Can you imagine anyone in their right mind following Peter? I told you he was impetuous... and I will bet you that he got the other apostles going as well. You see... sometimes our greatest fault is our greatest grace. It just has to be reversed and redirected. Impetuosity was Peter's downfall, but it was also his salvation.

Why... in the name of anything logical... would those men have left their nets and their fish to follow Jesus?

Why did they do it?

It does not make one ounce of sense. It was crazy.

Now, listen... do not be afraid of being crazy. Be afraid of not being bold. That is the one thing we have to fear.

There were moments when the impetuosity of Peter got the better of him. He had moments when he wished he had thought before he spoke. One such time was when Jesus talked about the Holy Eucharist, and Peter remarked, "Hey... come on now... this 'eat my flesh and drink my blood business...' we are getting a little carried away, are we not? Let us just stop this..."

And you can imagine, can you not, Jesus replying, "Do you want to go away or would you like to follow me, still?"

And Peter, in reply, asking, "Where are we going?"

I will bet you that there were nights when Peter thought to himself, "Did I do the right thing?"

Peter talked about fishing one more time in the Gospel. Do you know when that time was?

It was after the Resurrection.

All of a sudden everyone looked to Peter for leadership, for guidance. It happened after the moment when Mary Magdalene exclaimed, "He is not in the tomb! He is not in the tomb! He is not there... He has risen. I have seen it."

And all eyes went to Peter.

Why?

Because of what Jesus had spoken to Peter, *"Blessed are you Simon Bar-Jonah! For flesh and blood has not revealed this to you, but my Father who is in heaven. And I tell you, you are Peter, and on this rock I will build my church, and the gates of hell shall not prevail against it."*

Jesus will direct the grace of God that is in Peter... would you like to talk about making something out of nothing?

They all looked to Peter, because Jesus told them to. However, Jesus was not there, and the little infant Church, before it was truly born, looked to Peter for direction.   Do you recall what Peter said at that moment?

Read it in the Scripture... it is there in John 21:3.

Peter's response to the Resurrection and his newfound position as leader of the disciples was: *"I am going fishing!"*

We cannot conceive of Peter doing it... but he did.

Looks are deceiving. God can do all things. Look what He did with Peter.

Do you know Peter?

Well, of course you do.

He was a very old man. He had Parkinson's disease. The muscles in his face would not allow him to smile anymore; once what was a beautiful smile. He spent the last years of his life bent over in pain. Some people wished he were dead long before he died. Despite being bent and crippled with Parkinson's he fought for the life of the Church.

We do not call him Peter anymore. We called him "John Paul II" and now we call him "Benedict", but he is Peter. He is the holy father... the holy father is Peter.

Impetuousness can be a great grace. The world will tell you not to listen to your inspirations. People will tell you to be practical. The world will tell you that it is only your imagination you hear, when you hear a voice that speaks no words but only vibrations within. A voice that tells you to be holier... and better... and more forgiving... and more loving... and more prayerful. When the world tells you that what you are hearing is just your imagination, that it is not a real voice... like Peter... you must believe that IT IS THE VOICE OF GOD.

And as He called to Peter on the shores of the Sea of Galilee, He calls to us saying, *"Come, follow me!"*

Fr. Lavalley

For our sake He was crucified under Pontius Pilate; he suffered, died, and was buried...

Fourth Sunday in Ordinary Time

A reading from the Book of the Prophet Zephaniah:

Seek the Lord, all you humble of the earth, who have observed his law; seek justice, seek humility; perhaps you may be sheltered on the day of the Lord's anger. But I will leave as a remnant in your midst a people humble and lowly, who shall take refuge in the name of the Lord: the remnant of Israel. They shall do no wrong and speak no lies; nor shall be found in their mouths a deceitful tongue; they shall pasture and couch their flocks with none to disturb them.

A reading from the first Letter of Saint Paul to the Corinthians:

Consider your own calling, brothers and sisters. Not many of you were wise by human standards, not many were powerful, not many were of noble birth. Rather, God chose the foolish of the world to shame the wise, and God chose the weak of the world to shame the strong, and God chose the lowly and despised of the world, those who count for nothing to reduce to nothing those who are something, so that no human being might boast before God. It is due to him that you are in Christ Jesus, who became for us wisdom from God, as well as righteousness, sanctification, and redemption, so that, as it is written, "Whoever boasts, should boast in the Lord."

A reading from the holy Gospel according to Matthew:

When Jesus saw the crowds, he went up the mountain, and after he had sat down, his disciples came to him. He began to teach them, saying: "Blessed are the poor in spirit, for theirs is the kingdom of heaven. Blessed are they who mourn, for they will be comforted. Blessed are the meek, for they will inherit the land. Blessed are they who hunger and thirst for righteousness, for they will be satisfied. Blessed are the merciful, for they will be shown mercy. Blessed are the clean of heart, for they will see God. Blessed are the peacemakers, for they will be called children of God. Blessed are they who are persecuted for the sake of righteousness, for theirs is the kingdom of heaven. Blessed are you when they insult you and persecute you and utter every kind of evil against you falsely because of me. Rejoice and be glad, for your reward will be great in heaven."

At the time of this writing, I have been a priest in the parish of Saint Francis Xavier for sixteen years. Yet, I recall that when I first arrived I was so excited to learn that a parish school was also to become a part of my parish responsibilities. To this day, being the steward of the Saint Francis Xavier School continues to thrill me in so many ways.

Sixteen years ago I was sane enough to realize that running a parish school could be a hardship and a cross, but I always believed that having a parish school would benefit so many in so many ways and that it could remain a great joy for all who entered through its doors or who toiled at its periphery. Those of you who have been with me these past sixteen years may remember me addressing the potential of our parish school during my very first homily. Everything I spoke of sixteen years ago has remained true even to this very day.

I have been associated with the Catholic school system since I was in the fifth grade. I know the ins and outs of the Catholic school system. So... drawing from that well of experience there are a couple of things I would like to share with all of you.

Saint Francis Xavier School is a part of us and is a part of our community identity. The ownership of our parish school belongs, collectively, to two people. The first person to which it belongs is actually a group of people. It is you. It is me. It is the parish of Saint Francis Xavier.

The parish of Saint Francis Xavier has grown by leaps and bounds these past sixteen years. I have watched it grow as a father watches his infant child grow through the adolescent years into those of a teenager. It used to be that the parishioners of Saint Francis Xavier came exclusively from the city of Winooski, but it is not that way any longer. The parish of Saint Francis Xavier is so much more. Parishioners come to Saint Francis Xavier from all over the State of Vermont. They come from Winooski. They come from Burlington. They come from Colchester. They come from Essex. They come from Williston. They come from Milton, Jericho, Hinesburg, Shelburne, Bristol, etc... Parishioners come to Saint Francis Xavier from all over the place. But no matter where you live this is our place. Take pride in who we are.

Saint Francis Xavier is not just the parish with a school beyond the church parking lot. We are the parish with the school. Saint Francis Xavier School is part of us. It is part of our past. It is part of our present. It is part of our future. It is a part of who we are.

One hundred and forty years ago the Saint Francis Xavier school began with a little nun walking from Burlington to Winooski, along North Avenue, every day, without sidewalks. A little Sister of Providence traveled every day to a room within our parish to teach Catechism to our young people. That is how it all started, and we are still here. Saint Francis Xavier School is our school. We take pride in it.

There are many good schools in Vermont. There are many good schools in the communities that surround Winooski. It is not a question of competition. We have some wonderfully marvelous public schools in Vermont. We have some wonderfully dedicated public school teachers in Vermont. It is not about that, either. It is not about anything that ever tries to say, "We are better than you." It is just that we are different from public schools in many aspects; especially, in one aspect that comes to mind.

I can afford to be politically incorrect in my school.

I can walk into any room in my school and I can say, "You are loved by God."

I can walk into any room in my school and say, "Jesus Christ is truly present in the Holy Eucharist."

I can walk into any room in my school and say, "It is a beautiful thing to have devotion to the mother of God."

I can walk into any room in my school and say, "You need to be well prepared for the world, and you need to be good citizens," but I can also say to our students, "You need to be good citizens of Heaven."

I can do all of those things... and so can all of the teachers in our school.

It is the freedom to say what is forbidden in so many corners of our society these days. We can celebrate the birth of our Lord and Savior Jesus Christ with a Christmas pageant.

We can do that and so much more.

At the beginning of my visit with you this day, I pointed out the fact that the first person to which our school belongs is actually a collective group of people- us. There is another owner.

Three years ago we took our Saint Francis Xavier School and offered it to the hands of our Lady. We dedicated and consecrated our school to our Blessed Mother. From that moment on marvelous things have happened. Wonderful things have happened. Interest in our school has increased and we have been able to do things that we had once only been able to dream of doing. Incidentally, those things have happened, not with money from our parish, but with previously, unanticipated contributions. The size of our school building has increased and we have added programs.

In years past we have held open house events. Those events have been held for you. But you need not wait for such events to be scheduled, to be arranged. Everyone is invited to come to our Saint Francis Xavier School to look at the place, to walk through it, to see it, to speak with the teachers, to speak with the administrators, to speak with the children. It does not matter whether or not you have children attending our school. It does not matter whether or not you have children. The parish of Saint Francis Xavier is your parish. The Saint Francis Xavier School is your school. Come to us. Come visit us.

This very day I rededicate and reconsecrate the Saint Francis Xavier School to our Lady.

Presently, I would like to introduce you to two young ladies, Bridget Gagne and Angela Dupont. They are going to address their experience at Saint Francis Xavier School. When they are finished, however, I will come back to you, because you still have to hear about God's word. But, for the moment here are Bridget Gagne and Angela Dupont.

Hello. My name is Bridget Gagne and I am in the sixth grade. The most vivid memory I have of Saint Francis Xavier School is Miss Nancy Ryan. She is the best memory I have about the school. I have had many teachers that I've loved, but they are no longer at Saint Francis. Miss Nancy is still there. Miss Nancy is always there when I get hurt. She is there to give me my lunch tickets. She is also there to give me my Mom's and Dad's telephone number whenever I need to call them. Miss Nancy works at the front office so you can't miss her. One of the things I remember most about Miss Nancy is when I was in kindergarten. I was coming out of the bathroom and the door closed on my fingers. I screamed my heart out. My teacher came running and opened the door to get my fingers out. She took me to the nurse's office... that was when Miss Nancy came in and gave me Band-Aids and antibiotic cream. She made me feel better and I went back to class. A lot of people at Saint Francis are related to Miss Nancy. She is my friend's, Lauren, grandmother and Emily's aunt. They are also related to Autumn. If you are not related to Miss Nancy, she is your friend. Miss Nancy is like a best friend to each school kid. She was here before a lot of people were even born. We wouldn't even be having this school if she wasn't here. We all adore the hard work she puts into the school. Miss Nancy really makes this place neat to be at. She is very generous, kind, thoughtful, understanding, polite, and best of all a friend. Just let Miss Nancy know if you are having a hard time, do not feel well, or are hurt and she'll be there to help you one hundred percent. That is what Miss Nancy and Saint Francis Xavier School are all about.

My name is Angela Dupont and I am in the seventh grade. Catholic education is important to me, because it helps me become closer to God. It helps me to learn more about Him, so that I can become closer to Him. It teaches me that praying is very important and it can help people become better if they are sick, come back from or go to places safely, or it could be just because you love them and you want them to become closer to you. I also learn a lot about the Bible. We recently learned about the four evangelists: Matthew, Mark, Luke, and John. We learned about the order of the Bible. For example, we learned that the Book of Genesis comes before the Book of Exodus. I learned about all of these things in my religion classes. We learn, but at the same time we have fun. Catholic education has changed my life, because if I had never had religion classes I wouldn't have realized all of the great works of God, and also wouldn't have learned as much about the Bible. Without this Catholic education I wouldn't be me.

Miss Nancy... how does it feel to be declared a relic?

On this Fourth Sunday in Ordinary Time, we are preparing ourselves for Lent. And while I am not going to spend a great deal of time speaking about it this morning, because we are going to talk a lot about it during our next visit, I do want to mention a couple things about the Word of God given to us in today's readings.

As we read in the tribune, as we look around us, and as we read in contemporary newspaper articles there is much planning taking place concerning the future of our Diocese. That is just another way of saying the future of the Church in the State of Vermont is being discussed. It is alright to plan.

Much of the planning has to do with schedules and buildings, and that is alright as well.

Trying to prepare for our future is a fine thing to do, but we are the Church. And to be the Church is to be both a body and a bride at once: to be the body of Christ, and to be his bride. Such are the two mysteries Saint Paul spoke of through his writings.

Throughout the history of our Church... from its seed in its infancy beginning with Abraham... from Abraham through God's people, Israel... from the birth of Jesus to Pentecost, there have been changes of all kinds. There have been ups and there have been downs. We are going to have an ongoing discussion of such things throughout the Lenten season, but our discussion will always be framed through the lenses of our celebration of the pastoral mystery. What this means to us is that we see the passion of His death... His Resurrection... His Ascension... and the Ascension of the Holy Spirit into the Church... as an on-going reality. What this means is that there cannot always be a resurrection. A resurrection comes from death, from dying. There can be no resurrection without a death having occurred.

Whenever the Church has been renewed, two graces can be found at the very heart of that renewal, at the very core of the Church's renewal: repentance and holiness. Repentance and holiness in its members. If those two graces do not take place the rest falls away and the Church becomes tiny and is seemingly insignificant. And, that is alright, because bigger is not necessarily better. For this reason, if we are going to talk about a renewal, the renewal of you and the renewal of me, we must speak of our renewal as a part of an eternal journey.

In today's reading, Zephaniah speaks to us and says, *"Seek the Lord."*

Saint Benedict said that a monk was: One who seeks God.

That is what a Christian is. That is what a Catholic is: One who seeks God.

But Zephaniah tells us that the only people who will listen, who will seek God, are the humble of the earth. Zephaniah does not waste his words on people who will not listen.

"Seek the Lord, you humble of the earth."

What is a humble person?

One who is bashful...

One who is timid...

One who cannot speak...

No, all of those things are qualities of character, qualities of disposition.

Humility is a virtue. Humility is to know that one is totally dependent on God, either individually or collectively as a church. If the parish of Saint Francis Xavier does not know that it is totally dependent on God, then we are in trouble. If I do not know that I am totally dependent on God, then I am in trouble. If you do not know that you are totally dependent on God, then you are in trouble.

Humility is a virtue that allows us to know that even though we are broken and sinful the only place we need to go is to the lap of the Father.

That is where we need to go.

Then... Zephaniah tells us what a humble person does. A humble person observes His law. A humble person seeks justice. A humble person seeks humility. And the Lord will leave us as a remnant, as a little one.

Always be the little one. No matter how old you grow, be God's little one. That will put you in good stead with Him.

Shooting right from the hip, Saint Paul told the Corinthians who they were... and he started with chastising them with humility.

"Not many of you were wise by human standards."

Can you imagine how Saint Paul's admonishings to the Corinthians would go over today were he speaking to us... were he speaking to us as Americans?

It must be a part of our heritage, as Americans, for have you ever noticed that we think we have all the answers to everything? We know all the solutions. We are experts in every field. No one can tells us a thing. We have no need for a pope. Everyone of us believes we are infallible.

I remember being in conversation, not too long ago, with someone whose every sentence began with "I think... I think... I think... I think..." And then, it just came out of me. I could no longer help myself and ended up saying to him, "You know what your problem is? You don't think... you don't think... you don't think... You just react to what you want."

"Not many of you were wise by human standards, not many were powerful, not many were of noble birth. God chose the foolish of the world to shame the wise."

Crazy old saints. What weird people they were.

"God chose the foolish..."

Well, it is not hard in these modern days, in our society, to be among the foolish. Just mention to anyone that you go to church every Sunday or that you believe in God... you will find yourself placed in the fool's crowd right away. But, guess what... that puts you in a good place with God!

He chose the weak.

Well! I know one person in this church who is weak, and that is okay with me, because it is me. I know that. I read our opening prayer. We prayed for the grace to love God with our whole heart. Oh... there are so many places in my heart that are just plain selfish. Maybe that is why I need Lent.

The second thing we prayed for was for the grace to love all people. Ha! That is a good one. Do you know how that was stated? Our prayer was not just to love people. Our prayer was for the grace to love people the way God does.

I read a sign once that said, "Love your enemies... it will drive them crazy."

The Scripture's call to us is to boast in the Lord, to acknowledge the Beatitudes, to accept the Beatitudes.

Sometimes we get the impression of Jesus seating His disciples down on the ground in front of a blackboard and saying, "Now, I am going to teach you the Beatitudes. Number one: Blessed are the poor in spirit. Okay... memorize that one. Number two: Blessed are they who mourn..." And so on, and so forth.

Did He make up the Beatitudes the night before?

Did He think about them for a few days and nights?

Did He carry them around in His pocket for a while?

Or, did He create them for us right there, on the spot?

Jesus always looked at people in the face. And when He did, perhaps He saw someone who was broken in spirit; perhaps He saw someone who had been humiliated; perhaps He saw someone who had been rejected, someone not accepted. Perhaps all of that suffering showed in the eyes of those with whom Jesus spoke. Perhaps, it was into those eyes that Jesus looked and said, *"Blessed are the poor in spirit..."*

Blessed are you.

Perhaps Jesus saw someone returning from burying a loved one. Jesus would know that... His very presence brought comfort... He would notice eyes red with tears, *"Blessed are those who mourn..."*

Blessed are you.

And the timid and the shy who did not know whether or not they fit in with the crowd, *"Blessed are the meek..."*

"Blessed are those who hunger and thirst for righteousness..."

Perhaps He looked into the face of someone who had just forgiven a brother... or a sister... or an aunt... or an uncle... or a friend... or a neighbor... and Jesus called upon that which it took of that someone to forgive, and He saw the merciful person and said, *"Blessed are the merciful..."*

Blessed are you.

Perhaps He saw someone who was having a difficult time staying away from illicit relationships, but someone who was working very hard on it, but still having a difficult time. What an encouragement there could be if Jesus looked at one of God's children and said, *"Blessed are the pure in heart..."*

Blessed are you.

And then He gave that child of God a promise, *"Rejoice for you shall see God and your reward is great in heaven."*

Number one: Seek God.

That is what we pray for... to seek God.

Number two: Love other people as God does.

Number three: Start looking into people's faces.

Fr. Lavalley

On the third day he rose again in fulfillment of the Scriptures; he ascended into heaven and is seated at the right hand of the Father...

Fifth Sunday in Ordinary Time

A reading from the Book of the Prophet Isaiah:

Thus says the Lord: "Share your bread with the hungry, shelter the oppressed and the homeless; clothe the naked when you see them, and do not turn your back on your own. Then your light shall break forth like the dawn, and your wound shall quickly be healed; your vindication shall go before you and the glory of the Lord shall be your rear guard. Then you shall call, and the Lord will answer, you shall cry for help, and he will say: Here I am! If you remove from your midst oppression, false accusation, and malicious speech; if you bestow your bread on the hungry and satisfy the afflicted, then light shall rise for you in the darkness, and the gloom shall become for you like midday."

A reading from the first Letter of Saint Paul to the Corinthians:

When I came to you, brothers and sisters, proclaiming the mystery of God, I did not come with sublimity of words or of wisdom. For I resolved to know nothing while I was with you except Jesus Christ, and him crucified. I came to you in weakness and fear and much trembling, and my message and my proclamation were not with persuasive words of wisdom, but with a demonstration of Spirit and power, so that your faith might rest not on human wisdom but on the power of God.

A reading from the holy Gospel according to Matthew:

Jesus said to his disciples: "You are the salt of the earth. But if salt loses its taste, with what can it be seasoned? It is no longer good for anything but to be thrown out and trampled underfoot. You are the light of the world. A city set on a mountain cannot be hidden. Nor do they light a lamp and then put it under a bushel basket; it is set on a lampstand, where it gives light to all in the house. Just so, your light must shine before others, that they may see your good deeds and glorify your heavenly Father."

Let us talk about Lent.

The Lenten season is upon us. It arrives on Wednesday. It is not a fun time for Catholics. It is not supposed to be. It is not something to which we look forward, but it is a necessary part of our spiritual life.

Let us take a look at Lent.

Our goal is to avoid having a schizophrenic Lent. What do I mean by that...?

During Lent, Catholics do things or Catholics give up things. And that has everything to do with the birth and the death of Jesus Christ. Somewhere between the two experiences exists the life we live. Sometimes we think east is east and west is west, and never the twain will meet. Viewing our life through such a prism we believe that the death of Christ should not have anything to do with the birth of Jesus.

Well... if the one does not have anything to do with the other, then do not do it! There is no point to it..

The purpose for everything we do, during Lent, or for everything we give up, during Lent, is for the conversion of heart. We need a conversion of heart. If what we do or if what we give up during Lent does not change our lives, then what is the point?

So... we need to reintroduce ourselves to a word, an important word, and that word is: Occasion. We need to speak about the occasion of sin and the occasion of grace.

Now the Church has always told us that we must not put ourselves in the "occasion" of sin, because if we do we are in danger. Even to put ourselves in the "occasion" of sin, in and of itself, is a sin, because it is akin to walking on quicksand. We are so weak that we shall surely fall.

What is an "occasion" of sin?

An "occasion" of sin is those things that lead us into sin.

If I have a problem with lust, it might be good for me to get rid of pornography.

If I have a problem with drink, it might be good for me to give up alcohol.. and not just the act of going to a tavern.

If I have a problem with gossip or slander, it might be good for me to stay off the telephone or to change my friends.

In order for gossip or slander or detraction to take place two things are needed: I need a tongue and I need an ear. Remove one and the gossip or slander is gone.

If I am listening, I am contributing.

Let me say that again: "If I am listening, I am contributing."

Do you know what the scariest thing about sins against charity are?

We believe such things to be "just" gossip.

We believe such things to be "just" innocent detractions from our mundane lives.

There is no **just** about it. Gossip and slander are serious matters. Do not fool yourselves. People's reputations are serious matters. Gossip and slander are not loose; they are not light. The impact such things have on our lives goes to the very core of the Gospel.

The first thing we have to do is to look at ourselves and ask, "What is the "occasion" of sin in our lives?"

Now... I do not know about you, but I do not have to give that question much thought; I know the answer to that one. And to be perfectly honest with you, I would just as soon not think about the occasions of sin in my life, because I do not really want to avoid them. That is me being brutally honest with myself.

This is where grace enters our life. We cannot just leave a vacant spot where the "occasion" of sin is dispelled. We have to go to something else, and that to which we turn is the "occasion" of grace.

If you stand outside in the pouring rain, are you surprised to discover you are too soon soaked to the bone?

If you have light skin and summer comes, and you lay out in the sun for many hours on the first day of summer, are you surprised by the sunburn that will surely follow?

If you choose to not eat, are you surprised by the physical weakness and illness that will surely follow?

Each of those examples are occasions.

And just like those examples are "occasions" of sin... but the antithesis of sin's occasion is the "occasion" of grace. That is where Lent comes in.

If a salt shaker now contains pepper, but I wish it to contain salt once more, I had better rid the shaker of the pepper before refilling it with salt.

In the shaker of our being what will be the end result of us replacing the "occasion" of sin with the "occasion" of grace?

Here comes a scary little answer for you: ***We will belong to God.***

Would it frighten you to belong to Jesus?

After belonging to Jesus there is nothing left... only Jesus.

You see... we have to be careful, because we are Americans, and as Americans we have been programmed to think that nothing is good enough for us. We have been conditioned over and over and over again to believe that we need more of everything. We have been taught very carefully and have learned very well that we should never be inconvenienced.

The problem with greed is that there always needs to be more. It is like drinking salt water. Salt water will never quench thirst. We need to be careful of greed; terribly careful of greed.

Do you want to belong to Jesus Christ?

Then... that is to whom you must belong. There is no other.

Scripture says of God: *"I am a jealous God."*

God wants it all. Because God gave all.

So... we need to begin thinking about Lent, and speaking of the "occasion" of sin and the "occasion" of grace.

We must not fool ourselves.

We need to pray more.

Now... usually what we say at this point is, "I am so busy I do not have time to pray."

Let me suggest a radical idea to you. This is going to be a terribly radical idea to some of you; a terribly radical idea.

You say you do not have time to pray?

Turn off your television set.

How is that for a scary thought?

I do not know about you, but I can sit in front of a television set for three hours and at the end of three hours proclaim, "There is nothing on television!"

Well, whatever was I watching?

Have you ever done that?

Have you ever sat down and watched a program that you did not like the first time you saw it? Then... have you ever watched a rerun of that very same program as though it was going to turn out differently. Crazy, is it not?

You see... we need to have our televisions on, because if we do not have our televisions... if we do not have our stereo systems on... if we do not have all of the usual the background noise in our lives... the voice of God is going to whisper to us.

Oh yes... the voice of God speaks to you and speaks to me. He is forever telling us to, "Stop that!" and "Do this!" and "Do that!" and "Get close to me!"

All the while we are asking, "What about all of the rest?"

And Jesus is saying, "There is no *all of the rest*! There is only me."

You see... that is the problem with Jesus. He is one of those crazy suitors. He likes to go steady with one person. That one person is you.

Jesus does not want us to have distractions that keep us from Him. Now, that is not to say He does not want us to love other people. It is part and parcel of the same thing; but He does want us to give up things, and that is why it is so dangerous for us, because we are so hesitant to give up those things that do so very little to edify God or enhance our lives, really. We are constantly being told by the movers and shakers of our material world, "You deserve this or you deserve that..."

Here is a wonderful sentence we use when we buy something new or when we are given something new or when we acquire something new: "I really deserve this."

Have you ever used such a statement?

Have you ever been told, "Go on now, spend it. You really deserve it."

Have you ever said to yourself, "Gosh... I know I should not buy this, but I really deserve it."

Do you know what the real beauty of our faith is?

We do not get what we deserve!

Jesus, dying on the Cross, took care of that one!

There is time to pray. There is time to fast. There is time to give our attention to other people.

Listen to Isaiah, again... *Share your bread with the hungry, shelter the oppressed and the homeless; clothe the naked when you see them, and do not turn your back on your own... remove from your midst oppression, false accusation, and malicious speech.*

Do you think we need Lent or were we alright without it?

I am going to end today with a story. It is not an original story. A rabbi told this story to me. Rabbis have such wonderful stories. It is in their blood. They derived such ability through Jesus. Jesus told such wonderful stories.

There was a rabbi who was teaching his students and the rabbi said to them, "Inside of me there live two wolves. They dwell side by side in the depths of my being. Now, one wolf is ferocious. He is bloodthirsty. He is vicious. He is lustful. He is intemperate. He is selfish. He is angry. He cannot be trusted. There is blood on his jowls. He is a vicious, frightful animal; be careful if you ever meet him. He lives within."

"However... beside that wolf there lives another. This wolf is tame. He is quiet. He is docile. He is chaste. He is moderate. He is loving. He is a good wolf. There is nothing to fear from that one. Yet, the two wolves live within."

"The problem," the rabbi observed, "Is that only one of the wolves can survive. They cannot coexist as they are. One must survive and become strong, and the other must die."

One of the rabbi's pupils asked the rabbi, "Master, do you know which wolf will survive?"

"Oh, yes!" replied the rabbi. "Yes, I know which wolf will survive."

"Which one?" asked the pupil.

"The wolf that will survive," replied the rabbi, "Is the one I choose to feed."

Fr. Lavalley

He will come again in glory to judge the living and the dead, and his kingdom will have no end...

Ash Wednesday

A reading from the Book of the Prophet Joel:

Even now, says the Lord, "Return to me with your whole heart, with fasting, and weeping, and mourning; Rend your hearts, not your garments, and return to the Lord, your God. For gracious and merciful is he, slow to anger, rich in kindness, and relenting in punishment. Perhaps he will again relent and leave behind him a blessing, offerings and libations for the Lord, your God."

Blow the trumpet in Zion! Proclaim a fast, call an assembly; gather the people, notify the congregation; assemble the elders, gather the children and the infants at the breast. Let the bridegroom quit his room and the bride her chamber. Between the porch and the altar let the priests, the ministers of the Lord, weep, and say, "Spare, O Lord, your people, and make not your heritage a reproach, with the nations ruling over them! Why should they among the peoples, 'Where is their God?'"

Then the Lord was stirred to concern for his land and took on his people.

A reading from the second Letter of Saint Paul to the Corinthians:

Brothers and sisters: We are ambassadors for Christ, as if God were appealing through us. We implore you on behalf of Christ, be reconciled to God. For our sake he made him to be sin who did not know sin, so that we might become the righteousness of God in him.

Working together, then, we appeal to you not to receive the grace of God in vain. For he says: "In an acceptable time I heard you, and on the day of salvation I helped you. Behold, now is a very acceptable time; behold, now is the day of salvation."

A reading from the holy Gospel according to Matthew:

Jesus said to his disciples: "Take care not to perform righteous deeds in order that people may see them; otherwise, you will have no recompense from your heavenly Father. When you give alms, do not blow the trumpet before you, as the hypocrites do in the synagogues and in the streets to win the praise of others. Amen, I say to you, they have received their reward. But when you give alms, do not let your left hand know what your right hand is doing, so that almsgiving may be secret. And your Father who sees in secret will repay you.

"When you pray, do not be like the hypocrites, who love to stand and pray in the synagogues and on the street corners so that others may see them. Amen, I say to you, they have received their reward. But when you pray, go to your inner room, close the door, and pray to your Father in secret. And your Father who sees in secret will repay you."

"When you fast, do not look gloomy like the hypocrites. They neglect their appearance, so that they may appear to others to be fasting. Amen, I say to you, they have received their reward. But when you fast, anoint your head and wash your face, so that you may not appear to be fasting, except to your Father who is hidden. And your Father who sees what is hidden will repay you."

Most Catholics have heard the Ash Wednesday Gospel, many times, because many times we have set out together on our Lenten journey on Ash Wednesday. In today's Gospel the Lord was speaking to his first followers and through the preserved word He speaks to us. The Lord mentions three things of importance to us as we begin our Lenten journey. Perhaps we can think of His message to us as a sort of a three-fold program for us to follow during the next forty days. 1). Good deeds, 2). Prayer, and 3). Sacrifice.

Perhaps a good resolution for us to make on this Ash Wednesday is simply this: During each day of Lent try to do a good deed. Help someone in some way, no matter how small. Pray every day and make a sacrifice of self-denial.

Regarding self-denial, Catholics observe two rules or laws; the law of abstinence and the law of fasting.

The law of abstinence forbids the eating of meat on a day of abstinence. All Catholics, who have completed their fourteenth year, are bound by the law of abstinence. The days of abstinence are Ash Wednesday and all the Fridays of Lent.

The law of fasting has more to do with limiting the amount of food we indulge in on a given day than a complete abstinence of indulgence. Catholics are called to limit their food consumption, during days of fasting, to one full meal and two minor meals with no eating between meals. Catholics, who are between the ages of eighteen and fifty-nine are bound by the law of fasting. The days of fasting are Ash Wednesday and Good Friday.

In the bigger picture we are called to make sacrifices, willingly, and we willingly deny ourselves the pleasures of our usual routines because we seek to strengthen our spiritual selves by removing the clutter of our lives that serves to block out the voice of God. Through the inevitable discipline imposed upon us by good deeds, prayer, and sacrifice we find ourselves more open to the word of the Lord and, as a consequence, we become more spiritually alive.

The symbol of ashes has been with us for a long, long time. The ashes still remain a very strong symbol among Catholics. Many Catholics make a point of coming to mass on Ash Wednesday and receiving the ashes. The ashes are a sign or a symbol of death. The ashes serve to remind us that our eternal soul resides in a mortal vessel. We treasure life in this world, but we know that our life in this world will come to an end.

The importance of such awareness is to be concerned always with doing those things that are of eternal value; doing those things that will count once we have finished our lives in this world.

The message of Ash Wednesday is a somber one, but one borne of reality. Thus, when the gift of the ashes is bestowed upon you, a cross drawn in ashes is made upon your forehead, and these simple words are spoken:

Remember you are dust, and to dust you will return.

Fr. Searles

First Sunday of Lent

A reading from the Book of Genesis:

The Lord God formed man out of the clay of the ground and blew into his nostrils the breath of life, and so man became a living being.

Then the Lord God planted a garden in Eden, in the east, and placed there the man whom he had formed. Out of the ground the Lord God made various trees grow that were delightful to look at and good for food, with the tree of life in the middle of the garden and the tree of the knowledge of good and evil.

Now the serpent was the most cunning of all the animals that the Lord God had made. The serpent asked the woman , "Did God really tell you not to eat from any of the trees in the garden?" The woman answered the serpent, "We may eat of the fruit of the trees in the garden; it is only about the fruit of the tree in the middle of the garden that God said, 'You shall not eat it or even touch it, lest you die.'" But the serpent said to the woman, "You certainly will not die! No, God knows well that the moment you eat of it your eyes will be opened and you will be like gods who know what is good and evil." The woman saw that the tree was good for food, pleasing to the eyes, and desirable for gaining wisdom. So she took some of its fruit and ate it; and she also gave some to her husband, who was with her, and he ate it. Then the eyes of both of them were opened, and they realized that they were naked; so they sewed fig leaves together and made loincloths for themselves.

A reading from the Letter of Saint Paul to the Romans:

Brothers and sisters: Through one man sin entered the world, and through sin, death, and thus death came to all men, inasmuch as all sinned for up to the time of the law, sin was in the world, though sin is not accounted when there is no law. But death reigned from Adam to Moses, even over those who did not sin after the pattern of the trespass of Adam, who is the type of the one who was to come.

But the gift is not like the transgression. For if by the transgression of the one, the many died, how much more did the grace of God and the gracious gift of the one man Jesus Christ overflow for the many. And the gift is not like the result of the one who sinned. For after one sin there was the judgement that brought condemnation; but the gift, after many transgressions, brought acquittal. For if, by the transgression of the one, death came to reign through that one, how much more will those who receive the abundance of grace and of the gift of justification come to reign in life through the one Jesus Christ. In conclusion, just as through one transgression condemnation came upon all, so, through one righteous act, acquittal and life came to all. For just as through the disobedience of the one man the many were made sinners, so, through the obedience of the one, the many will be made righteous.

A reading from the holy Gospel according to Matthew:

At that time Jesus was led by the Spirit into the desert to be tempted by the devil. He fasted for forty days and forty nights, and afterwards He was hungry. The tempter approached Him and said to Him, "If you are the Son of God, command that these stones become loaves of bread." He said in reply, "It is written: One does not live on bread alone, but on every word that comes forth from the mouth of God." Then the devil took Him to the holy city, and made Him stand on the parapet of the temple, and said to Him, "If you are the Son of God, throw yourself down. For it is written: He will command his angels concerning you and with their hands they will support you, lest you dash your foot against a stone." Jesus answered him, "Again it is written: You shall not put the Lord, your God, to the test." Then the devil took Him to a very high mountain and showed Him all the kingdoms of the world in their magnificence, and he said to Him, "All these I shall give to you, if you will prostrate yourself and worship me." At this, Jesus said to him, "Get away, Satan! It is written: The Lord, your God, shall you worship and him alone shall you serve." Then the devil left him and, behold, angels came and ministered to him.

This day is the first Sunday of Lent, and if you did not get started on your Lenten journey on Ash Wednesday... start today.

The Church, on this first Sunday of Lent, shares with us a wonderful reality. She begins with the Book of Genesis: The Beginning.

The Book of Genesis is wonderful reading. To be quite honest with you, however, it is not much of a science book. But, it never was intended to be a science book. When you read the Book of Genesis, do not read it with a critical, scientific eye. Look for theology. The theology in the Book of Genesis is great.

The Book of Genesis does not tell much at all about how our world was created... the authors did not know; such is the business of science. The Book of Genesis is not concerned with **how** God did something. The Book of Genesis is concerned with **what** God did. The text of the Book of Genesis has not been scribed to tell us how the heavens go, but how to go to Heaven. The purpose of the Book of Genesis is very clear; it is a family tree of sorts. And so, through today's reading we are going to trace our DNA, in a manner of speaking. We are going to trace our lineage back to the very first Dad and the very first Mom, persons whom we call Adam and Eve.

Before we talk about Adam and Eve, there is one thing that must be made very clear. It is paramount. If we are going to follow Jesus into the desert, through our reading of the forty days and forty nights He spent fasting in the wilderness before being tempted by the Devil, our understanding is paramount. We need to grasp and embrace one very important thing from the Book of Genesis. It is the first line of our reading from the Book of Genesis: *The Lord God formed man out of the clay of the ground and blew into his nostrils the breath of life, and so man became a living being.*

What does that one line tell us?

It tells us that we belong to God.

We are God's handiwork.

How we were created is not important. The fact that we were created is.

The fact that we were created by God is important.

When we read the Book of Genesis, and learn of everything that was created by God, we are going to know that God saw what He had made and *God saw that it was good.*

God saw what He had created: *And God saw that it was good.*

God saw what He had created was good until He gets around to the creation of man in his own image. At that point, in the Book of Genesis, God's observation of His creation changes. *And God saw everything He had made, and behold, it was very good.*

Imagine God thinking of us that we were very good...

Perhaps He saw something in us that we do not see. God was pleased with His handiwork, and His handiwork became, not only His creation, but His children.

His children.

We belong to God.

We must always go back to that truth. We are His. We are children of God.

We belong to God.

We do not belong to God as you or I would own a set of golf clubs, a lamp, or any other material possession. We are His beloved children. With all of our brokenness, all of our sinfulness, all of our frailty, and all of our foolishness, we are His.

We belong to God.

And when He looks at you, and when He looks at me, He always says the same thing, "You are mine... you are mine... oh heavens... you there... you are mine."

Whenever God says, "You are mine...", He also says, "I love you."

In the Creation narrative, given to us by the Book of Genesis scribes, we discover something very important and germane about Adam and Eve, and about ourselves. Let us look back, then, and see how much we have changed over the centuries.

Where did God place Adam and Eve?

We commonly name that place: Paradise. We call it the Garden of Eden. No matter how we choose to refer to it, the important thing here is that Paradise is a state of happiness.

What did God give to Adam and Eve?

He gave them an abundance. They have been given everything. Adam and Eve received it all.

Now, there was just one tiny stipulation that Adam and Eve received from God, and that stipulation was: "Leave this one tree alone. It is not for you. This one particular tree is mine. But.. that really should not bother you, because I have given you the orchard."

Was that particular tree any better or more special than the others? Not really. But, God declared it off limits to Adam and Eve.

You shall not eat of the fruit of the tree that is in the midst of the garden, neither shall you touch it, lest you die.

But for some crazy reason, what Adam and Eve wanted most was the one thing God said not to touch.

Have we changed all that much?

Neither shall you touch it...

If I had a stack of envelopes, each one of them containing five hundred dollars, and I said to you, "You may each have one envelope, but only one per customer. However, there is one envelope among the stack of envelopes that you may not have or even look inside. It is the envelope without any writing on it."

At the very least, would you not want a peek into it?

Even if the envelope holds nothing...?

Why?

Because human nature is such that we are inclined toward feeling that something labeled as being off limits to us is somehow better than those things we already possess.

We have not changed much, have we?

The Book of Genesis teaches us much about human nature. More, perhaps, than we sometimes care to know.

Saint Thomas Aquinas taught that a person cannot choose sin as long as the choice being made is seen as being sinful. Saint Thomas Aquinas had a wonderful expression he often used. He said, "We never choose evil, as evil; we choose evil as the apparent good."

"We never choose evil, as evil; we choose evil as the apparent good."

Far too often we say to ourselves, "If it looks good, it must be good for us. It looks good, therefore, it must be good."

We talk ourselves into it, "If it feels good, do it."

The best example I ever saw of original sin, the best example I can remember, was the very first movie I ever saw. It was _Snow White and the Seven Dwarfs_. My mother took me to see it.

Have you ever seen the movie, "Snow White"?

I was fascinated by the witch in the movie. I recall being extremely bothered by the fact that this particular character put herself through a myriad of trials, simply because she wanted to be the fairest of them all. But the consequence of her endeavors was that she turned herself into a witch and that meant she was never going to be pretty again. There was no antidote to her witchiness.

Do you remember what the witch did next?

The witch concocted a plan to destroy Snow White.

And what did she come up with as an enticement for Snow White?

It was an apple.

Do you remember the part in the movie where the witch filled her cauldron with all manner of vileness and awful things, and set it to boiling?

At long last she dipped the apple into the cauldron.

Do you remember what the apple looked like when she lifted it out of the cauldron?

It looked like a skeleton. The witch looked at the apple and asked, "Does it have an antidote?"

With those old, gnarled fingers she held the apple up for all to see and asked, "Does it have an antidote?"

Do you remember what the antidote to the poisoned apple was?

It was love's first kiss.

Love's first kiss would destroy eternal death.

Now, think of your own life and think of love's first kiss; love's first kiss from the tree upon which our Lord and Savior Jesus Christ was crucified.

I recall, so vividly, the scene of the witch, the cauldron, and the apple. It terrified me. I crawled onto my mother's lap and clung to her neck at that point. I was twenty-one at the time... not really!

We are only attracted to sin when sin is made to look good; when sin is made to feel good.

Back in the Garden of Eden, Eve bit the apple.

Now, let us take a moment to reflect on how far we have come... on how much we have grown spiritually, emotionally, and intellectually from the first parents.

My heavens... when one sins, what is the first thing that needs to be said?

It is, of course, simply this, "I have sinned and I am sorry. Please forgive me."

But that is not what happened in the Garden of Eden, is it?

Misery loves company. Eve took a bite of the apple. Then, she handed the apple to Adam and said, "It is wonderful, here have a bite."

Misery loves company.

Adam reacted marvelously to this situation too, didn't he? What a gentleman. What was Adam's lament before God?

"She made me do it."

Ladies, whether you like it or not, chivalry died on that day.

Eve was no better before God, either. On that day, in the garden of Eden, Eve became the original Flip Wilson. Do remember what Flip Wilson was fond of saying before his audiences?

"The Devil made me do it!"

Well, sometimes the Devil does make you do it, but let us not lay blame for everything we do at the feet of that ole boy. We are pretty darn good at sinning on our own.

Saint Thomas Aquinas taught that temptation comes from three sources: the World, the Flesh, and the Devil.

Soon after reading of Adam's and Eve's eating of the fruit of the tree in the midst of the garden, we read of their banishment from the Garden of Eden. And shortly thereafter, we read of awful things that happen to them and to their family. Not long after we read of the birth of Cain and Abel, we read of the first murder... and we are still killing our brothers and sisters.

Sometimes we cannot even wait until our brothers and sisters are free from the womb, can we?

Have we changed all that much?

No, not really.

President Harry Truman had a sign on his desk in the Oval Office that read: The Buck Stops Here.

Sorry Harry... the buck stops with Jesus on the Cross.

You see... sometimes we forget that God breathed life into us. Sometimes we forget that we belong to Him.

On the other hand, God never forgets that we belong to Him, and therein is found the beauty of our faith: God does not forget who we are.

We forget.

God never stops loving us.

Fast forward into the desert with Jesus.

We need to have a grasp on what it means to be in the desert, because despite what it looks like outside of our windows, each and every day of our lives, you and I are in the desert. So is our Church; so is our world.

The desert within which we find ourselves is not one of sand dunes and arid landscape. The physical desert is very hot by day and very cold by night. The physical desert is inhabited by snakes and scorpions and jackals, and, oh yes... our friend the wicked wolf... he is there too.

The first property of our desert, however, is abandonment. It is a state of being alone, without a compass and without a sense of direction. In our desert, we hunger and we thirst, but not for water and not for bread. We are hungry and thirsty for only those things that God can provide. The state of our desert is loneliness. It is fearfulness. It is being afraid of getting up in the morning and afraid of going to bed at night. It is being haunted with the memory of past sins and it causes us to wonder if God really cares about us.

That is the desert of which I speak. Do you know it?

Have you felt it?

Together with all of that... there is someone else in our desert. He does not look human. He is not human. He looks and acts much like the ravenous wolf we spoke of the last time you and I were together.

He has piercing eyes. He hides from our sight. He does not come out in public, because he knows he would frighten us and we would run away. But... he watches us. And he watches us when the discouragement and the despair and the sinfulness and the fear of not having God's mercy are beset upon us. And when those fears are upon us, he is there... ready to strike. He is ravenous.

If you and I were taking a journey through a jungle, we would hire someone who knew the jungle. Our guide would go before us with a machete and would clear a path for us to follow. Our guide would know the jungle and would protect us from danger.

That is what Jesus did.

He went first.

He went into the desert, because He knew we had to go there. That is why He fought with the horrible beast. The beast who only springs when he knows we are weak. He sprang when Jesus was weak, but Jesus conquered him, because Jesus trusted His Father.

If you and I are going to get anything at all out of Lent, we must be silent everyday. We must set aside a bit of time, you, for yourself, and me, for myself, to be alone with our thoughts, to be alone with God. Inside each of us there exists a little contemplative that craves silence; silence to be alone with God, so that we can hear God can speak. We need to nurture our contemplative; we all do.

Do not be afraid of being quiet, and do not be afraid of being in the desert. And those pair of eyes... the eyes of the beast... do not be afraid of them, either. At the very beginning I made mention of one very important thing. Do you remember what that one thing was?

Here it is again: You belong to God.

Keep telling yourself that: You belong to God.

You are His.

Look beyond the beast. Do not stare at him in the eyes. Do not play with him. Turn in the other direction. There is another pair of eyes in the desert longing to meet your gaze.

He went before us.

He is still there.

He waits for us

His name is Jesus.

And do you know why He is there?

Because we are...

Fr. Lavalley

We believe in the Holy Spirit, the Lord, the giver of Life, who proceeds from the Father and the Son...

Second Sunday of Lent

A reading from the Book of Genesis:

The Lord said to Abram: "Go forth from the land of your kinsfolk and from your father's house to a land that I will show you. I will make of you a great nation, and I will bless you; I will make your name great, so that you will be a blessing. I will bless those who bless you and curse those who curse you. All the communities of the earth shall find blessing in you." Abram went as the Lord directed him.

A reading from the second Letter of Saint Paul to Timothy:

Beloved: Bear your share of hardship for the gospel with the strength that comes from God.

He saved us and called us to a holy life, not according to our works, but according to his own design and the grace bestowed on us in Christ Jesus before time began, but now made manifest through the appearance of our savior Christ Jesus, who destroyed death and brought life and immortality to light through the gospel.

A reading from the holy Gospel according to Matthew:

Jesus took Peter, James, and John his brother, and led them up a high mountain by themselves. And He was transfigured before them; His face shone like the sun and His clothes became white as light. And behold, Moses and Elijah appeared to them conversing with them. Then Peter said to Jesus in reply, "Lord, it is good that we are here. If you wish, I will make three tents here, one for you, one for Moses, and one for Elijah." While he was still speaking, behold, a bright cloud cast a shadow over them, then from the cloud came a voice that said, "This is my beloved Son, with whom I am well pleased; listen to Him." When the disciples heard this, they fell prostrate and were very much afraid. But Jesus came and touched them, saying, "Rise, and do not be afraid." And when the disciples raised their eyes, they saw no one else but Jesus alone.

As they were coming down from the mountain, Jesus charged them, "Do not tell the vision to anyone until the Son of Man has been raised from the dead."

The second Sunday of Lent means that we are well into our Lenten journey. There are many journeys in the divine Scripture. There is the journey of Jesus into the desert. There are the journeys of God's people, traveling from one resting place to another. But on this second Sunday of Lent, we are called to reflect on the journey of God's people as given to us in the story of the Exodus. It is yet another story of God's people traveling; of God's people trusting in God. We are all asked to journey and to travel, but today our journey continues with a reading from the Book of Genesis, and with a little fellow named Abram. Who was Abram and why is he important?

Abram is recorded as being the first person to whom God officially spoke. Abram had no religion, because religion did not exist in those days. In Abram's time, people worshiped as best they could from their heart. That was all they had... God had not spoken to His children, yet.

When God finally spoke, He spoke to a fellow named Abram. Now, later on in the Scripture Abram will become Abraham, because in Jewish theology when you change someone's name, you change their destiny. Abram will become Abraham. Who was Abram?

Abram was a desert dweller. He was a sheik. He belonged to a little tribe of people. He had no children, but he took care of his band of people. Abram's people were bedouins. They were nomads. Eventually, it was to that man of the desert whom God would speak.

Abram had no clue as to whom God was, and that is important, for when God spoke to Abram, God was a stranger to him. Abram did not know our God. Under the best of circumstances, it would appear to be risky business paying heed to a voice that appears in one's head, or however it was that God came to Abram. Be that as it may, Abram was selected by God to be the beginning of God's people. Abram was destined to become the head of the Jewish people. Eventually, the seed planted by God would blossom into our Church.

So begins our story. It is the beginning of our history.

When God spoke to Abram, God entered into a covenant with him.

Now... a covenant is nothing more than a contract and we enter into contracts all of the time the simplest of which is: I will give you this, if you give me that. For example, if you give me your check, I will give you my house. If you want to pay on a bank note for a while, you will get a car out of it. There is much of this, for that. Contracts between people are signed. Both parties to a contract must sign the contract. But the covenant between God and Abram is a holy contract. There was nothing to sign.

God said to Abram, "Here are the things I am going to give to you. I am going to give you a son, (Abram was childless at this point).   I am going to give you a people. They are going to be more numerous than the stars in the sky. I am going to give you a land to live in, the Holy Land, and for your part, what I am going to ask of you is that you know me as your only God; that you put your total trust in me- Total trust."

Do you know what the signing of the contract between God and Abram reads?

"I will be your God and you will be my people."

"We belong to each other."

That is why it is so important for us to reflect on those things that happened all those many years ago; to remember our roots; to remember from whence we came.

Then, God said to Abram, (and this is a little tough), "It is time you left home. I want you to leave your house, your tribe, and your land. I want you to leave your father's house. I want you to go where I lead you."

Well, that is not very easy, is it? For the most part, human beings do not like change. Even when change is for the better we find change difficult. We like what is familiar. Even when we are not happy with what is familiar, we still find comfort in that which is familiar. One can live in misery for centuries.

Change takes courage and change takes trust.

When a little child learns to walk it needs to leave the security of a chair or a bench, but it always goes towards something, (usually not just off into space), but into the arms of a parent. The first step we take, takes trust. It takes trust and it takes letting go.

Once upon a time there was a wall of stone and there was a man climbing that wall of stone. The man almost made it to the top, but as he reached for the top of the cliff he lost his grip and he lost his balance. He fell. As he was falling, his arms were flailing and as luck would have it one of his hands latched onto a root protruding from the face of the cliff. Having arrested his fall thusly, he held tightly onto the root protruding from the face of the cliff, and though he was suspended hundreds of feet above the base of the cliff, for the moment he was safe.

Can that be done...? Sure, it can... Harrison Ford did it all the time when he was Indiana Jones.

But there he was... hanging from a root... just like Harrison Ford. Below him was certain death, and above him there was nothing that would lend itself to the man for climbing out of such a predicament.

Have you ever found yourself in a similar situation?

Have you ever found yourself in a seemingly impossible situation?

Well... when we find ourselves in such difficult moments... when there is no conceivable way out of our trials and tribulations... what do we learn how to do?

In those moments, we learn how to pray... do we not?

And we learn how to pray passionately... do we not?

And we make promises to our God that we too soon forget once the danger has passed... do we not?

Well, that is precisely what our hapless mountain climber did.

Hanging onto the root for dear life and he cried out to our Lord, "Dear God, will you please come and rescue me!"

All of a sudden he heard a voice, and The Voice simply replied, "Yes."

Now... the man was so startled at that moment, he almost let go of the root right there and then.

The man called out once more, "Hello...?"

Again, The Voice replied, "Yes."

The man asked, "Who's there?"

"Who did you want to talk to?" The Voice asked.

"I was calling to God," replied the man.

"You have my attention," replied The Voice. "What do you want?"

"Will you save me?" asked the man.

And God said, "Of course I will save you. That is what I do. I save. You have been in a mess since the Creation of the World. I always save. That is my nature."

The man enthusiastically replied, "That is wonderful! That is great!" However, he continued to hang by the root and nothing happened.

"God..." the man called out.

"Yes..." God replied.

"I thought you were going to save me."

"I am going to save you, " God said. "But, you need to make the first move."

"What do you mean," asked the man. "I cannot move. I am stuck here."

"Oh..." God replied. "Just let go of the root."

The man thought about that for a minute and began, "I beg your pardon..."

"Let go of the root."

"Why would I do that?"

"Because your hand needs to be free so I can grab onto it."

The man asked, "Can you grab me by my wrist or by the nape of my neck or by my hair, instead?"

God said, "No... I want your hand. For the instant you let go will prove to me you trust me. The instant you let go I will grab onto your hand and I will pull you to safety. Besides, you cannot hang onto that root forever."

"Then I will do it..." replied the man. "But can I ask you one more question first?"

God said, "Yes... one more question... but be quick about it as we are running out of time."

The man looked toward the top of the cliff and asked, "Is there anyone else up there?"

There is no one else.

There does not need to be.

God is enough.

God is enough.

God will lead us where we need to go.

To be sure... it certainly is rough at times. It is not always easy. The Gospel does not always console.

Oh... the Gospel consoles plenty, but it also challenges us. Listen to Paul, speaking to Timothy, in today's second reading.

Bear your share of hardship for the gospel...

Saint Paul loved Saint Timothy. Saint Paul was like a father to Saint Timothy. We can see that in Paul's letters. Saint Timothy was like a son to Saint Paul.

Bear your share of hardship for the gospel...

Bear your share of the hardship. There is no cotton candy here. Ours is not a powder puff God. He is a God who loves us infinitely and works to get us home where we belong.

Bear your share of hardship for the gospel...

Let us turn to the holy Gospel according to Saint Matthew for today's third reading and see what is going on in there. It is the Gospel of the Transfiguration.

The Transfiguration is a very strange event, because it is the only time in the Gospels when we read of anything like this occurring. Jesus never let His Divinity shine through... except for this one time- the Transfiguration.

In order to understand the Transfiguration we have to know where Jesus was before this occurred.

Jesus had been with Peter, James, and John. He said to them, "Listen to me. I have to go to Jerusalem. I will be betrayed. I will be handed over to the authorities. I will be made to suffer greatly."

Peter said, in reply, "Don't go to Jerusalem."

In His heart, Jesus was probably saying, "It is not just about you, Peter. It is about the whole world. The people of the world need me."

Jesus wanted to prepare Peter, James, and John for what was to come. And the Gospel tells us *...His face shone like the sun and His clothes became white as light.*

Jesus dazzles. And that is a very strange thing, because Divinity hides itself. One of the best games God plays with us is hide and seek. He loves it. He hides in disguises, usually in people. Sometimes it is very difficult to see Him, as it is in the Host. Yet, we know that in that little wafer of bread Jesus is present: Body and Blood. However, in this particular event His Divinity shined through. It needed to, in order to prepare them for the sacrifice to come- His death on the Cross.

It did not work... they would forget.

Jesus was not alone on the mountain with Peter, James, and John. Moses and Elijah were there, as well. And there, at that most wonderful of moments, what happened?

Peter happened.

What a mouth!

Peter... what a wonderful, wonderful saint! But, what a piece of work with whom the Lord took it upon Himself to work. Peter was forever opening his mouth and sticking his foot in it. He made promises he could never fulfill. He was always embarrassing himself, and he always had to be in charge. He always had a better idea than anyone else. In reality most of his ideas were horrible ones.

So, there they were... high upon that mountaintop... Moses and Elijah, Peter, James, and John... and Jesus was shining like the sun. Who must be the one to break the silence?

The fisherman.

Peter.

"Lord, it is good that we are here. If you wish, I will make three tents here, one for you, one for Moses, and one for Elijah."

Peter might as well have said, "I can build three condos here. One for you... one for Moses... and one for Elijah. Never mind the rest of the world, we could just stay here forever."

Cozy... right?

At that moment, upon that mountaintop... Peter had a plan, but the problem with his plan was that it was a very self-centered plan. What God is going to do with Peter, eventually, is positively wonderful, because Peter became the head of the Catholic Church... when God finished with him. But, we are not there, yet. At that moment and upon that mountaintop God had not even begun to start transforming Peter.

If I had been tasked with selecting the leader of the Disciples, Peter would have been the last person I would have chosen. It may come as a surprise to you for me to say this... but the only one of Jesus' disciples, who was qualified to lead, was Judas. Judas would have been my choice.

Look how much trouble we would be in, if such a choice would have been mine to make.

God knows best.

It is amazing what God can do with us.

What God did with Peter was simply amazing.

At any rate, high upon that mountaintop Peter was babbling on and on about his plan for building tents, and about all of them staying on top of that mountain, and about all of them getting away from the rest of the world, (of course, if they stayed there Jesus would not have gone to Jerusalem)... when, all of a sudden, a cloud came upon them and they became afraid. And a voice came out of the cloud and spoke to them saying, *"This is my beloved Son, with whom I am well pleased; listen to Him."*

Perhaps one translation of that event could be: "Peter knock it off. You are here to learn, not to teach. You are here to be turned into an apostle, not a builder. We do not need any tents. We need hearts in love with Christ."

That is, after all, what we need.

Peter always tried to run away from the Cross, until the end.

Did you know there was a time when the Church was being persecuted and Peter, who was at that time the Pope, was running away from Rome? He was running away from persecution, and, upon the Appian way, Jesus came to him and asked, "Peter, where are you going?"

Peter replied, "I am getting out of town. Where are you going Lord?"

And Jesus said, "I am going back to be crucified anew."

Peter said, "No... I will go back."

Do you know how Peter was crucified?

Upside down.

Do you know why Peter was crucified upside down?

Because Peter said that he was not worthy to die like his master.

Peter turns out okay...

Never give up on yourselves. God is not finished with you, yet.

But, you have to be quiet.

This is my beloved Son, with whom I am well pleased; listen to Him.

Listen to Him. Read His Scripture. Listen to His Church. Listen to the Holy Father. All of these are who we are.

And then, they were scared... and then, they were frightened... and all of a sudden ...*they fell on their faces and were terrified.*

And what happened next was such a beautiful thing.

Do you recall what happened next?

Not a word.

A hand.

He touched them.

They looked up and they saw Jesus, only; no more light; no more glow; no more clothes as white as light- just Jesus.

They saw a Jewish man among other Jewish men. He was probably a little scruffy. They did not bathe much back then. They had been out on the road for a while. His hair was probably more than a little tangled than we are used to seeing it depicted, not appearing as we see in pictures. His beard was probably in need of a trim. But His hand... He touched them.

Do you recall what it was He said to them?

Rise, and have no fear.

"Do not be afraid."

"It is me."

Do not be afraid.

What does Jesus say when He rises from the dead?

To Magdalene... to Peter, again... to James... to John, Jesus said, "Do not be afraid. It is me. It is going to be alright."

Without the dazzle... without the glow... it is Jesus. He is here.

And as long as we know that... we are going to be alright.

So... I have to know, (and I suspect you do, as well), there are going to be things in our lives that we will have to let go of... like Abram in our first reading, today. You see... God does not want us to live in fear or in despair or in depression or in anger or in hatred. God wants us to be at peace, and that means there are things we must leave behind us. And we are not going to leave those things unless and until we follow some- one.

I like the dazzling Jesus... but the dazzling Jesus is very rare.

So, what do we see?

Looking up... what do we see?

We see a light that never burns out. We see Jesus, who is with us in the blessed Sacrament. We see Jesus, who comes to us in the Mass. We see Jesus on the Altar.

And what does all of that say to us?

It is very simple, really.

Rise, and have no fear.

Do not be afraid.

Fr. Lavalley

With the Father and the Son he is worshiped and glorified...

Third Sunday of Lent

A reading from the Book of Exodus:

In those days, in their thirst for water, the people grumbled against Moses, saying, "Why did you ever make us leave Egypt? Was it just to have us die here of thirst with our children and our livestock." So Moses cried out to the Lord, "What shall I do with this people? A little more and they will stone me!" The Lord answered Moses, "Go over there in front of the people, along with some of the elders of Israel, holding in your hand, as you go, the staff with which you struck the river. I will be standing there in front of you on the rock in Horeb. Strike the rock, and the water will flow from it for the people to drink." This Moses did, in the presence of the elders of Israel. The place was called Massah and Meribah, because the Israelites quarreled there and tested the Lord, saying, "Is the Lord in our midst or not?"

A reading from the Letter of Saint Paul to the Romans:

Brothers and sisters: Since we have been justified by faith, we have peace with God through our Lord Jesus Christ, through whom we have gained access by faith to this grace in which we stand, and we boast in hope of the glory of God. And hope does not disappoint, because the love of our God has been poured out into our hearts through the Holy Spirit who has been given to us. For Christ, while we were still helpless, died at the appointed time for the ungodly. Indeed, only with difficulty does one die for a just person, though perhaps for a good person one might even find courage to die. But God proves his love for us in that while we were still sinners Christ died for us.

A reading from the holy Gospel according to John:

Jesus came to a town of Samaria called Sychar, near the plot of land that Jacob had given to his son Joseph. Jacob's well was there. Jesus, tired from his journey, sat down there at the well. It was about noon.

A woman from Samaria came to draw water. Jesus said to her, "Give me a drink." His disciples had gone into the town to buy food. The Samaritan woman said to him, "How can you, a Jew, ask me, a Samaritan woman, for a drink?" For Jews use nothing in common with Samaritans. Jesus answered and said to her, "If you knew the gift of God and who is saying to you, 'Give me a drink,' you would have asked him and he would have given you the living water." The woman said to him, "Sir, you do not even have a bucket and the cistern is deep; where can you get this living water? Are you greater than our father Jacob, who gave us this cistern and drank from it himself with his children and his flocks?" Jesus answered and said to her, "Everyone who drinks this water will be thirsty again; but whosoever drinks the water I shall give will never thirst; the water I shall give will become in him a spring of water welling up to eternal life." The woman said to him, "Sir, give me this water, so that I may not be thirsty or have to keep coming here to draw water."

Jesus said to her, "Go call your husband and come back." The woman answered and said to him, "I do not have a husband." Jesus answered her, "You are right in saying, 'I do not have a husband.' For you have had five husbands, and the one you have now is not your husband. What you have said is true." The woman said to him, "Sir, I can see you are a prophet. Our ancestors worshiped on this mountain; but you people say that the place to worship is Jerusalem." Jesus said to her, "Believe me, woman, the hour is coming when you will worship the Father neither on this mountain nor in Jerusalem. You people worship what you do not understand; we worship what we understand, because salvation is from the Jews. But the hour is coming, and is now here, when true worshipers will worship the Father in Spirit and truth; and indeed the Father seeks such people to worship him. God is Spirit, and those who worship him must worship in Spirit and truth." The woman said to him, "I know that the messiah is coming, the one called the Christ; when he comes, he will tell us everything." Jesus said to her, "I am he, the one speaking with you."

At that moment his disciples returned, and were amazed that he was talking with a woman, but still no one said, "What are you looking for?" or "Why are you talking with her?" The woman left her water jar and went into town and said to the people, "Come see a man who told me everything I have done. Could he possibly be the Christ?" They went out of the town and came to him. Meanwhile, the disciples urged him, "Rabbi, eat." But he said to them, "I have food to eat of which you do not know." So the disciples said to one another, "Could someone have brought him something to eat?" Jesus said to them, "My food is to do the will of the one who sent me and to finish his work. Do you not say, 'In four months the harvest will be here'? I tell you, look up and see the fields ripe for the harvest. The reaper is already receiving payment and gathering crops for eternal life, so that the sower and the reaper can rejoice together. For here the saying is verified that 'One sows and another reaps.' I sent you to reap what you have not worked for; others have done the work, and you are sharing the fruits of their work."

Many of the Samaritans of that town began to believe in him, because of the word of the woman who testified, "He told me everything I have done." When the Samaritans came to him, they invited him to stay with them; and he stayed there two days. Many more began to believe in him, because of his word, and they said to the woman, "We no longer believe because of your word; for we have heard ourselves, and we know that this is truly the savior of the world."

Indeed, only with difficulty does one die for a just person, though perhaps for a good person one might even have the courage to die. But God proves His love for us in that while we were still sinners Christ died for us.

God proves His love for us.

And there she was... the woman at the well. The woman of Samaria. A nameless woman with so much to teach us. You see... Jesus simply had to get to her, so she could get to Him. There are no mistakes in the Providence of God. It is all in God's plan, even those events that appear to us as being accidental in nature.

Jesus broke all of the rules. In those days, He could have gotten into big trouble for His interaction with the woman of Samaria. The Scribes and the Pharisees could have had a heyday. They probably did. And so too the Samaritans. Now, let us take a look at it.

On this third Sunday of Lent, we are given the Gospel according to Saint John. And throughout Saint John's gospel, he speaks to us about sacraments. Sacraments, sacraments, sacraments. Over and over again. And we always know we are going to be given two words: Water and Bread. Those two words are going to come up all of the time: Water and Bread; cleansing and life; banquets overflowing. But, today we are handed a little glass of water.

There is a very important line in today's reading. It can be the easiest thing to get... or the easiest thing to overlook if we are not careful. So, I am going to show you what I believe is the most important indication of what is going on within the text of the entire reading. The line to which I direct your attention is only four words long: *It was about noon.*

Saint John was not in the business of telling us the time just for the sake of letting us know what time it was.

It was about noon.

To begin with... we read of Jesus and His apostles traveling outside the usual circles. They have traveled out of their way and should not have been near a Samaritan town in the first place. Neither of them should have gone into the Samaritan town, but they were hungry and needed that which the town had to offer. Why was it that Jesus stayed behind and did not go into the town to get food with the rest of the apostles?

Could it have been that Jesus did not want to be seen in the Samaritan town... or was His encounter with the Samaritan woman destined?

Was Jesus deliberately waiting for her?

In reality, the Samaritan woman was broken. She needed Jesus. However, she was not aware that she needed Him.

It was about noon...

Why is that such an important line?

Because no one goes to the well at noon.

The well was a very important place for villages in those days. In those days one did not travel to a mall for coffee and one did not dish the dirt at the local fast food restaurant. Such places did not exist. On the other hand, the well was an oasis for villagers. They replenished their household water stores at the well. Who retrieved the water from the well?

The women of the village did.

Their's was a very chauvinistic society. The women of the village always went to the well, but going to the well was advantageous for it provided women with a respite from the routine of household life. Going to the well provided a respite from family, from cleaning, from cooking, from laundry, etc. When one went to the well for water, one did not go to the well just for the water. The well provided an opportunity to dish, as well.

The well was a good place to talk. The well was a good place to exchange ideas; to exchange recipes, perhaps. "What is going on with the family?   What is going on next door? What is going on down the street? What is going on in so and so's life?"

The well was a good place to gossip. It was a good place to tell tales out of school. In many ways, the well was a fun place to be.

There were two times of the day when villagers went to the well: Before the sun came up, and after the sun went down. Going to the well at other times meant drawing hot water from the well. Well water rose in the coolness of dawn and just after sunset.

No one, who was in the know, went to the well at noon.

The well was a gathering place in the early morning and early evening. Those were the times to go to the well. The only reason for going to the well at noon was that one could be sure that no one else would be there.

Why would a person want no one else to be at the well?

Well... if one was labeled by the others, she would not want anyone to be there.

If one was shunned by the others, she would not want anyone to be there.

If one was snubbed by the others, for they saw her as wicked, she would not want anyone to be there.

If one were the object of ridicule and laughter and gossip about having five husbands, and now about finding a new guy, she would not want anyone to be there.

The woman of Samaria was shamefaced. She did not want anyone to see her.

There is a tremendous difference between shame and guilt. A good dose of guilt never hurt anyone. If I push you down and you say, "Why did you do such a bad thing?" and I say to you in reply, "Don't put a guilt trip on me!" Well, I should have a guilt trip put upon me, should I not?

Clearly, I have done something wrong, but that something can be rectified. I can apologize to you. I can make amends. I can be determined not to do such a thing, again. Such doings are akin to the conditions of a good confession.

Guilt is a good person admitting to doing something bad.

Shame, on the other hand, is allowing your sin to cling to you like molasses or tar.

Try to cleanse yourself of such things.

Shame says, "Of course I did a bad thing, what else could I do I am an evil person."

Shame says, "There is no hope for me."

Shame says, "I am a wretched human being."

Shame says, "I am nothing."

Shame is not of God. It is not of Jesus. It is not of the Gospel.

And that was why the woman of Samaria so desperately needed Jesus.

So, there she was... the woman at the well. The woman of Samaria. And there she was at noon... but oh-oh... on that day there was someone else at the well. Someone was going to see her. But, at the same time she observed that the person at the well was not from Samaria; at least, she did not recognize Him. And as she drew closer to the well she resigned herself to filling up her water jug anyway. Then, she realized that the person standing by the well was a Jew. "Oh my God... it's a Jew. It's a Jew!"

That made things even worse.

In those days, Jews did not have anything to do with Samaritans. Jews were not allowed to talk with Samaritans. A Jew was not even allowed to touch a Samaritan's utensils. Jews were not allowed to have anything to do with Samaritans, at all.

However, the Jewish man standing next to the well spoke to the woman of Samaria and said, "Will you give me a cup of water?"

The Samaritan woman was shocked.

She replied by asking, "You are a Jew, and you are asking me, a Samaritan, for a cup of water?"

"Yes," He said. "I am thirsty."

What did Jesus have for the woman of Samaria in exchange for her cup of water?

He has Living Water.

He has the Water of Baptism.

He has the Water of Forgiveness.

He has the Water of Mercy.

He has the Water of Compassion.

He has the Water of the Holy Spirit.

With His water He can remove all the mud and tar from the Samaritan woman. He can make her whole once more.

The woman of Samaria began by calling Him a Jew, she ended by calling Him: Messiah.

Jesus wanted to heal her. Jesus needed to heal her. But to heal her there had to be an admission of guilt on her part.

Jesus needed to get in there to lance her wound.

So, Jesus said to her, *"Go call your husband and come back."*

She replied, *"I do not have a husband."*

What Jesus was saying there is... "I am going to forgive you, but you have to 'fess up. Bring it forth. Let me see the wound."

Jesus said, *"You are right in saying, 'I do not have a husband.' For you have had five husbands, and the one you have now is not your husband. What you have said is true."*

And before we get to the good stuff in Saint John's Gospel, we are treated to a theological debate on the part of the Samaritan woman, (for me that is where this particular Gospel gets boring).

"Where is the best place to worship? On the mountain, in the hills, in the valleys... where do we go? Let us talk theology. Let us not talk about guilt, mercy, and forgiveness."

Did you notice how the Gospel gets a bit heavy in there?

After a while, do you find yourself kind of hoping to just get through it? Especially after reading it all these years...

I love the story of Jesus and the Woman of Samaria, but the ensuing interplay evades the issue before us.

Let us talk about forgiveness.

Let us talk about Living Water.

She was healed.

And, what was the very next thing she did?

She did what everyone does whosoever has really and truly found Christ.

When one has truly found Christ, one becomes an evangelist by and through the very way one lives. One becomes an evangelist, a teacher of religion, an apostle of the Good News.

So, what did she do?

She headed right back into town.

Did she walk?

No. She ran. She was traveling so fast she left her jug behind.

"Come and see what I have found!" she proclaimed. "Come and see who I have found!"

It is amazing, is it not... she did not want to keep the knowledge of Jesus all to herself. She wanted to share. She could hold her head up high, once more. He gave her forgiveness and restored her dignity. No more labels would be applied to her.

Can you imagine what they used to call her?

A tramp, perhaps. A whore. A hundred different labels... vile labels.

My God how well we label one another... labels to correspond with every letter in the alphabet.

There were no more labels for her. And in her love for Jesus, she brought the villagers out to see Him. But, remember that for Samaritans to interact with Jews was unheard of. However, the Samaritans did return to the well with her and they asked one question of this particular Jew. Of course, they were certain the answer would be, "No."

"Will you come and stay with us for a while?"

"Yes."

With that one answer, Jesus broke through all kinds of barriers, traditions, and laws.

He will break through anything to get to us. That is who He is.

He will break through any barrier to get to us. There are no barriers for the Sacred Heart. There is only the Sacred Heart.

And He went into the village of Samaria.

We need Him to come into our villages... into our homes... into our lives... to sit by our wells.

In the opening prayer we prayed, "Lord, do not let us be overcome by our weakness, but let us be consoled by your love."

There she was... the woman at the well... the woman of Samaria. Nameless.

We never see her again.

Or do we?

I have never been certain of such things... I cannot prove my suspicions... there is no way to verify what I suspect to be true... but I have always wondered, "Does the nameless woman of Samaria simply disappear at the end of this particular Gospel passage?

Is that really the end of her association with our Lord and Savior?

There are other nameless women in the Gospel.

Do you recall the woman with the jar of alabaster... the precious perfume... who washed His feet?

Was it her?

Do you remember the women on the way to Jerusalem... the Way of the Cross?

Was the woman of Samaria among them?

What about the woman with the veil, who wiped the face of Jesus?

Could it be the woman of Samaria?

What about the women at the foot of the Cross?

Was she among them?

What about the women at the empty tomb?

Are we talking about one woman... two women... four women... five, six, eight, ten?

How many are there?

It matters not.

Whether there is one or one million... or as many heads as we could count in our Church, today... one Savior is enough for all. And our Savior comes to each of us, individually.

Here we sit beside our own wells... our wells of hope... our wells of despair... our wells of longing... our wells of fear... our wells of sin... our wells of virtue... our wells of emptiness... our wells of prayerfulness... our wells of guilt... and our wells of forgiveness... Here we sit at high noon waiting and waiting. And we put out our hand and we call out, "Sir... sir... sir..."

He takes us by the hand saying, "I am here. It is me. Jesus."

Fr. Lavalley

He has spoken through the Prophets...

Fourth Sunday of Lent

A reading from the first Book of Samuel:

The Lord said to Samuel: "Fill your horn with oil, and be on your way. I am sending you to Jesse of Bethlehem, for I have chosen my king from among his sons."

As Jesse and his sons came to the sacrifice, Samuel looked at Eliab and thought, "Surely the Lord's anointed is here before him." But the Lord said to Samuel: "Do not judge from his appearance or from his lofty stature, because I have rejected him. Not as man sees does God see, because man sees the appearance but the Lord looks into the heart." In the same way Jesse presented seven sons before Samuel, but Samuel said to Jesse, "The Lord has not chosen any one of these." Then Samuel asked Jesse, "Are these all the sons you have?" Jesse replied, "There is still the youngest, who is tending the sheep." Samuel said to Jesse, "Send for him; we will not begin the sacrificial banquet until he arrives here." Jesse sent and had the young man brought to them. He was ruddy, a handsome youth to behold and making a splendid appearance. The Lord said, "There... anoint him, for this is the one!" Then Samuel, with the horn of oil in hand, anointed David in the presence of his brothers; and from that day on, the spirit of the Lord rushed upon David.

A reading from the Letter of Saint Paul to the Ephesians:

Brothers and sisters: You were once darkness, but now you are light in the Lord. Live as children of light, for light produces every kind of goodness and righteousness and truth. Try to learn what is pleasing to the Lord. Take no part in the fruitless works of darkness; rather expose them, for it is shameful even to mention the things done by them in secret; but everything exposed by the light becomes visible, for everything that becomes visible is light. Therefore, it says: "Awake, O sleeper and arise from the dead, and Christ will give you light."

A reading from the holy Gospel according to John:

As Jesus passed by he saw a man blind from birth. His disciples asked him, "Rabbi, who sinned, this man or his parents, that he was born blind?" Jesus answered, "Neither he nor his parents sinned; it is so that the works of God might be made visible through him. We have to do the works of the one who sent me while it is day. Night is coming when no one can work. While I am in the world, I am the light of the world." When he had said this, he spat on the ground and made clay with the saliva, and smeared the clay on his eyes, and said to him, "Go wash in the Pool of Siloam." So he went and washed, and came back able to see.

His neighbors and those who had seen him earlier as a beggar said, "Isn't this the one who used to sit and beg?" Some said, "It is," but others said, "No, he just looks like him." He said, "I am." So they said to him, "How were your eyes opened?" He replied, "The man called Jesus made clay and anointed my eyes and told me, 'Go to Siloam and wash.' So I went there and washed and was able to see." And they said to him, "Where is he?" He said, "I don't know."

They brought the one who was once blind to the Pharisees. Now Jesus had made clay and opened his eyes on a Sabbath. So then the Pharisees also asked him how he was able to see. He said to them, "He put clay on my eyes, and I washed, and now I can see." So some of the

Pharisees said, "This man is not from God, because he does not keep the Sabbath." But others said, "How can a sinful man do such signs?" And there was a division among them. So they said to the blind man again, "What do you have to say about him, since he opened your eyes?" He said, "He is a prophet."

Now the Jews did not believe that he had been blind and gained his sight until they summoned the parents of the one who had gained his sight. They asked them, "Is this your son, who you say was born blind? How does he now see?" His parents answered and said, "We know that this is our son and that he was born blind. We do not know how he sees now, nor do we know who opened his eyes. Ask him, he is of age; he can speak for himself." His parents said this because they were afraid of the Jews, for the Jews had already agreed that if anyone acknowledged him as the Christ, he would be expelled from the synagogue. For this reason his parents said, "He is of age; question him."

So a second time they called the man who had been blind and said to him, "Give God the praise! We know that this man is a sinner." He replied, "If he is a sinner, I do not know. One thing I do know is that I was blind and now I see." So they said to him, "What did he do to you? How did he open your eyes?" He answered them, "I told you already and you did not listen. Why do you want to hear it again? Do you want to become his disciples, too?" They ridiculed him and said, "You are that man's disciple; we are disciples of Moses! We know that God spoke to Moses, but we do not know from where this one is from." The man answered and said to them, "This is what is so amazing, that you do not know where he is from, yet he opened my eyes. We know that God does not listen to sinners, but if one is devout and does his will, he listens to him. It is unheard of that anyone ever opened the eyes of a person born blind. If this man were not from God, he would not be able to do anything." They answered and said to him, "You were born totally in sin, and you are trying to teach us?" Then they threw him out.

When Jesus heard that they had thrown him out, he found him and said, "Do you believe in the Son of Man?" He answered and said, "Who *is he, Sir, that I may believe in him?" Jesus said to him, "You have seen him, and the one speaking with you is he." He said, "I do believe, Lord," and he worshiped him. Then Jesus said, "I came into this world for judgement, so that those who do not see might see, and those who see might become blind."*

Some of the Pharisees who were with him heard this and said to him, "Surely we are not also blind, are we?" Jesus said to them, "If you were blind, you would have no sin; but now you are saying, 'We see,' so your sin remains."

Let us look at the Word of God.

The Scripture readings on this the fourth Sunday of Lent are all about light and darkness. They are about seeing, but they are also about hearing. Perhaps, they are connected in someway such that the hearing helps the seeing. At least, maybe, the hearing focuses the seeing.

The first thing we want to do is to look at today's first reading, because what is contained within that reading is so important for us and for our spiritual journey... as a church... as a diocese... as individuals. We need to pay close attention to what is contained within the text of that first reading, and, if we do, we will discover anew that God does not think the way we do.

There was a wonderful prophet. His name was Samuel. Samuel was so obedient and did his job so very well. And the reason he did it so well is because he was always listening to what God was saying to him; he never misquoted God; he never gave his own interpretation of God's word.

God said to Samuel, "Go down to Jesse's. Jesse has many sons, and from one of those sons I am going to select a king for Israel. And I want you to take the horn of the chrism, the anointing oil. I want you to take it with you, because we are going to anoint a king. Now, you go down to Jesse's house. He has fine sons. Go on down there. You are not going to vote or elect. I will point out who the next king will be."

Samuel went down to Jesse's house, and saw many, fine, strapping, young men. But God said, "They are all very nice, but no... no... no... no... and no thank-you."

Samuel asked Jesse if he had any more sons who might be considered. And Jesse pointed out the fact that his youngest son was still out working in the fields, but Jesse assured Samuel that his youngest son was certainly not fit to be a king. He was too young and too inexperienced, and, beside all of that, Jesse thought he had already shown Samuel the cream of the crop. But Samuel said, "Let us go out to the field."

Jesse's youngest son was ruddy and handsome to behold; and when they saw the young man standing in the field tending his sheep God said, "That is the one. That is David, King David; of the line of David; of the household of David."

Samuel, being very obedient, went down right away, took the chrism, poured the oil on David, and anointed him King of Israel. David was God's choice.

And so are you.

And so am I.

You were anointed with chrism. Probably most of us were anointed twice. Father Ragis and I were anointed three times. You were anointed at Baptism, and that means you belong to God. Your anointing means that you are His child and you were baptized into His priesthood, into His kingship. You were baptized into the wonderful vocation of spreading the Word of God. You were anointed. You were God's choice.

Now, how does it work?

For that answer, let us go to the Gospel.

I never taught English and I never taught Journalism, but I love stories. And if I had the opportunity to sit down with Saint John, and possessed the grace to correct his work, I would do it. I would have looked at the Gospel reading we had today, (if it were fiction), and I would have said, "Look, you have too much here."

"Saint John, you have a beautiful story here, but you are filling it up with gobbledegook."

I do not know about the rest of you, but I could not wait to get to the end of Saint John's Gospel, today. There is all kinds of stuff in there and I felt compelled to take out my magic marker and say, "Nope... nope... nope... nope... cut that out... go ahead and leave that in... you do not need that in there... It is getting kind of depressing here, so cut that part out... and remove that part, as well. Now, Saint John, let us rewrite the story and let us see how it should look."

Having rewritten the story with Saint John, to suit my personal preferences, here is how my version would have looked.

There was a man who was born blind. And the poor man suffered without sight. And, because of the philosophy of the time, the people believed he was a great sinner and God had cursed him. And if not he... well at least his parents were great sinners. So already we have put the scarlet A upon the whole family. Because of his lack of sight this blind man had nowhere to go, but somehow, either through friends or by his own hands, he found himself at the feet of Jesus. Jesus looked at him and took pity upon him. And Jesus did what every kid who plays baseball does. Jesus spit in his hands. Divine saliva. Jesus picked up earth. It is good earth. It was made by His Father. Jesus made a mud pie out of His saliva and His Father's earth. He took the mud pie and He smeared the eyes of the man born blind, saying, "Now, go wash in the Pool of Siloam."

And here is how my version of the story would have ended.

The man returned from washing his face and he could see. And all of the people, and all of the Scribes, and all of the Pharisees, and all those who lived in Jerusalem and Israel went before Jesus and proclaimed His

divinity. "Hosanna son of David... thank God we have the Messiah. Look
at what He has just done. He has given sight to the blind. God is with us!
This is Emmanuel!" And they all lived happily ever after.

Would not that have been a better story... without all of the gobbledegook?

But, you see... Saint John's Gospel is not fiction. And I could never
and would never correct Saint John, because he did not inject the gobbledegook. They did... they did.

How sad.

The Scribes and the Pharisees were extremely legalistic. They were
filled with rhetoric. They were overflowing with self-righteousness. And to
all of that they added a measure of jealousy that was terribly invasive.
They had extreme, excessive pride. When Jesus healed the man born
blind, the Scribes and the Pharisees did not applaud. They did not proclaim His divinity. They did not celebrate. Instead, they did an awful
thing.

Do you recall, from the Gospel according to Saint John, what they
called Jesus?

They said He was a sinner.

They called Jesus a sinner.

They called the Word Incarnate... the second person of the Blessed
Trinity... the Son of God... they called Him a sinner.

They called Him a sinner.

On that day one man gained sight; everyone else was blind.

Now... one can go blind from natural causes; one can go blind from
external forces. But one can also will blindness upon himself. I could
make a vow right this moment to close my eyes and to never open them
again. I would be living in darkness, would I not?

I can also stick my fingers in my ears, so that I do not hear.

There is a willful blindness and a willful deafness in this world. And at that moment, not too far from the pool of Siloam, as the world became bright for one man, others chose to live in darkness.

When you call Jesus "sinner" the lights go out!

When you call Jesus "savior" they go on.

The Pharisees and the Scribes threw him out... the man who had once been blind. They did not even rejoice in his sight. How blind can one be! But when they threw him out Jesus sought out the man right away.

Given the mind set of the Pharisees and the Scribes, it was probably not very safe for the two of them to be seen together. That did not bother Jesus. Such things never did. He always has to get to us... no matter what.

Jesus always has to get to us, no matter what.

And Jesus always stays with us, no matter what.

The man, who had been blind, looked up and saw Jesus, a man whom he had never seen before. He had just felt His thumbs. Now, there was going to be another miracle. The man, who had been blind, was going to get double vision. He received vision of the eyes, soon he was going to receive vision of the soul.

"Do you know who the Son of Man is," the man asks. "I want to believe in Him."

"He is standing right in front of you."

To look into the face of Jesus... to see His face... to hear His word... to open our eyes... to open our mouths.

And so, here is the choice: To see or not to see; To hear or not to hear; To accept or not to accept.

Come Holy Spirit, fill the hearts of your faithful.

Maybe the first vision we have to see is our self. I suspect that when we really see our self through the eyes of faith we will become both terrified and overjoyed, all at once.

We will become terrified, because we will realize we need a savior, and that we are not nearly as good as we believe ourselves to be. We have a long way to go. Perhaps we need to say, "Oh Lord that I may see."

We need to see Jesus everywhere and in everything we do. From the moment we rise, to the moment we return to bed, we need to see Jesus in every corner of our lives.

And, we will be overjoyed in knowing that no matter how far away we seem to be, and no matter how far it seems we have to go, Jesus loves us. He is here for us.

With His clay formed from saliva and earth... with His bread and with His wine... with His water and with His oil... Jesus is here for us.

We live in a world full of enticements, a world full of distractions. Let us pray for His thumbs... and then look up... and in looking up we will see Jesus.

Fr. Lavalley

We believe in one holy Catholic and Apostolic Church...

Fifth Sunday of Lent

A reading from the Book of the Prophet Ezekiel:

Thus says the Lord God: "Oh my people, I will open your graves and have you rise from them, and bring you back to the land of Israel. Then you shall know that I am the Lord, when I open your graves and have you rise from them, O my people! I will put my spirit in you that you may live, and I will settle you upon your land; thus you shall know that I am the Lord. I have promised, and I will do it."

A reading from the Letter of Saint Paul to the Romans:

Brothers and sisters: Those who are in the flesh cannot please God. But you are not in the flesh; on the contrary, you are in the spirit, if only the Spirit of God dwells in you. Whoever does not have the Spirit of Christ does not belong to him. But if Christ is in you although the body is dead because of sin, the spirit is alive because of righteousness. If the Spirit of the one who raised Jesus from the dead dwells in you, the one who raised Christ from the dead will give life to your mortal bodies also, through his Spirit dwelling in you.

A reading from the holy Gospel according to John:

Now a man was ill, Lazarus from Bethany, the village of Mary and her sister Martha. Mary was the one who had anointed the Lord with perfumed oil and dried his feet with her hair; it was her brother Lazarus who was ill. So, the sisters of Lazarus sent word to Jesus saying, "Master, the one you love is ill." When Jesus heard this he said, "This illness is not to end in death, but is for the glory of God, that the Son of God may be glorified through it." Now Jesus loved Martha and her sister and Lazarus. So when he heard that he was ill, he remained for two days in the place where he was. Then after this he said to his disciples, "Let us go back to Judea." The disciples said to him, "Rabbi, the Jews were just trying to stone you, and you want to go back there?" Jesus answered, "Are there not twelve hours in a day? If one walks during the day, he does not stumble, because he sees the light of this world. But if one walks at night, he stumbles, because the light is not in him." He said this, and then told them, "Our friend Lazarus is asleep, but I am going to awaken him." So the disciples said to him, "Master, if he is asleep, he will be saved." But Jesus was talking about his death, while they thought that he meant ordinary sleep. So then Jesus said to them clearly, "Lazarus has died. And I am glad for you that I was not there, that you may believe. Let us go to him." So Thomas, called Didymus, said to his fellow disciples, "Let us go to die with him."

When Jesus arrived, he found that Lazarus had already been in the tomb for four days. Now Bethany was near Jerusalem, only about two miles away. And many of the Jews had come to Martha and Mary to comfort them about their brother. When Martha heard that Jesus was coming, she went to meet him; but Mary sat at home. Martha said to Jesus, "Lord, if you had been here, my brother would not have died. But even now I know that whatever you ask of God, God will give you." Jesus said to her, "Your brother will rise." Martha said to him, "I know that he will rise, in the resurrection on the last day." Jesus told her, "I am the resurrection and the life; whoever believes in me, even if he dies, will live, and everyone who lives and believes in me will never die. Do you believe this?" She said to him, "Yes, Lord. I have come to believe that you are the Christ, the Son of God, the one who is coming into the world."

When she had said this, she went and called her sister Mary secretly, saying, "The teacher is here and is asking for you." As soon as she heard this, she rose quickly and went to him. For Jesus had not yet come into the village, but was still where Martha had met him. So when the Jews who were with her in the house comforting her saw Mary get up quickly and go out, they followed her, presuming that she was going to the tomb to weep there. When Mary came to where Jesus was and saw him, she fell at his feet and said to him, "Lord, if you had been here, my brother would not have died." When Jesus saw her weeping and the Jews who had come with her weeping, he became perturbed and deeply troubled, and said, "Where have you laid him?" They said to him, "Sir, come and see." And Jesus wept. So the Jews said, "See how he loved him." But some of them said, "Could not the one who opened the eyes of a blind man have done something so that this man would not have died?"

So Jesus, perturbed again, came to the tomb. It was a cave, and a stone lay across it. Jesus said, "Take away the stone." Martha, the dead man's sister, said to him, "Lord, by now there will be a stench; he has been dead for four days." Jesus said to her, "Did I not tell you that if you believe you will see the glory of God?" So they took away the stone. And Jesus raised his eyes and said, "Father, I thank you for hearing me. I know that you always hear me. I know that you always hear me; but because of the crowd here I have said this, that they may believe that you sent me." And when he had said this, he cried out in a loud voice, "Lazarus, come out!" The dead man came out, tied hand and foot with burial bands, and his face was wrapped in a cloth. So Jesus said to them, "Untie him and let him go."

Now many of the Jews who had come to Mary and seen what he had done began to believe in him.

The fifth Sunday of Lent hails the rapid approach of the Feast of Easter. Thus, we should really take advantage of the last couple of weeks of Lent. Do not slack off. Devote more time to prayer, to penance, to alms giving, and to all of those things the season calls for us to do.

Have you noticed how considerably lengthy the Scripture readings of the past three weeks have been? The readings have been lengthy, but they are also deeply significant. In reality, they are a trilogy. The Scripture readings of the past three weeks have a common theme running through them.

For the third Sunday of Lent, we read about the woman of Samaria... a nameless woman at a well... a woman who was isolated, alone, and drenched in sin. She was offered water... not water from the well... but Living Water by our Lord and Savior Jesus Christ.

For the fourth Sunday of Lent, we read about a man born blind. He lived as the nameless woman at the well did... in isolation... in loneliness and abandonment. And in referring to his blindness, he was accused of being born in sin.

For the fifth Sunday of Lent, we read about Lazarus. One could not become any more isolated than Lazarus in death. Of being entombed... that is real isolation.

Aside from the isolation depicted therein, each of those readings have something in common. In all three readings there are people, who, at the beginning of their stories, encounter a Jewish man and encounter God in that Jewish man. A journey of the soul takes place in each of them. He appears as Jesus, but His appearance manifests itself as Lord. When it can be proclaimed that Jesus is Lord, marvelous things begin to happen.

The readings of the past three Sundays are taken from the Gospel of Saint John. Because they are of Saint John's Gospel, each of the readings reflect Sacrament. So... mindful of that reflection... let us take a look at today's reading.

There is much taking place in today's Gospel reading. There is much humanness taking place, but there is a tremendous amount of divinity that transcends today's Gospel reading, as well. Let us set the scene and let us see what is happening, shall we...

The characters in today's Gospel reading were not strangers to Jesus. They are Mary, Martha, and Lazarus. Their home was Jesus' home away from home. It is quite obvious, through our reading of Martha's conversation with Jesus, that Jesus is well known to them, because Martha is speaking about the resurrection of life on the last day and she would not have known anything about all of that were it not for her intimate association with Jesus in Bethany. Such conversations must have flowed between Jesus and Martha, as table talk, for her to have had even a clue as to what the resurrection of life on the last day was all about.

Suddenly, something very tragic happened in that little house in Bethany. Lazarus, Mary's and Martha's brother, became gravely ill. In response to that illness, they did what anybody in their shoes at that time would have done... they dispatched someone to return with Jesus right away.

A messenger was dispatched to inform Jesus of Lazarus' illness. Mary and Martha were confident Jesus would return right away, because Lazarus was His friend. Lazarus is even described in today's Gospel reading as the one whom Jesus loves. And that takes us to the craziest part of this Gospel reading. A messenger found Jesus and told Him that Lazarus was gravely ill and Jesus responded by saying, more or less, "I love him. I care for him. I am going to stay here for two more days."

Have you ever noticed how we run around frantically when people get sick; frantically rushing about trying to find one cure or another?

Jesus did not.

Jesus responded to the news of His friend's illness by remaining *for two days in the place where he was.*

Did you ever stop to think that maybe Jesus needed to pray for two more days?

Sometimes we rush into things, because we so passionately want to make things right. We want to save the ones we love. So... we rush right in there because we think we have all the right words; we think we possess the where-with-all to make things right.

There is one thing I have learned from my years in the priesthood, but it came to me much later than earlier. Would you like to know what that one thing is?

It is one thing to go into a situation, but it is quite another thing to be sent.

It is one thing to go into a situation, but it is quite another thing to be sent.

What we need to learn from our Gospel reading today is that things happen in God's time. Things happen in God's way. And sometimes we do not take enough time to pray about things. On the other hand, when we take the time to pray... we do not get a vision... we get a push... and that push is called Actual Grace. You will know when it is time to move... after you have prayed and become saturated in Actual Grace.

That is what Jesus was doing in today's Gospel reading.

Alright... so Jesus finally traveled to Bethany.

Are you ready for the humanness I spoke of earlier?

Martha met Jesus.

Can you perceive the coldness of her tone when she speaks to Him?

"...if you had been here my brother would not have died."

Burrrrr...

What would you and I have done were we the recipients of those words, at that moment?

Well, perhaps in one way or another we would have replied, "Oh I am so sorry. I really did not realize how bad it was. That was so thoughtless of me. Please forgive me. I am sorry I was late."

But Jesus did not respond that way at all. Nope. He did not apologize for being on God's timetable. Jesus goes when His Father sends Him. Not a minute before.

Rather than apologizing to her, Jesus challenged Martha.

"Your brother will rise again."

"Well, I know he will, Martha replied. "On the last day, but I still know you can do something."

Hey... by the way... where was Mary. Why was she not there with Martha and Jesus?

Mary was back home. Why?

I believe there is one appropriate word we could use to describe Mary's absence from that scene: Pouting.

You would think the proper thing to do would have been to go to meet Jesus... would you not? After all, you sent for Him.

Martha attempted to save the day. Secretly taking Mary aside she said, "Jesus is asking you to come."

No... He did not!

Jesus did not ask any such thing.

All of that business was Martha trying to move things along. Martha learned a lot from that point onward. Let us give her some credit, shall we...

Two lines are repeated in today's Gospel reading. When Mary finally arose and went to where Jesus was, she said, *"Lord, if you had been here, my brother would not have died."*

She said the very same thing her sister Martha said upon meeting Jesus. It is the same line. *"Lord, if you had been here, my brother would not have died."*

The other line that is repeated twice in today's Gospel reading is this: *"Jesus became perturbed."*

Even Jesus gets perturbed. Does that not make the connection between you and me and Jesus a little more heartfelt?

Why was Jesus perturbed?

Because of their lack of faith. Because of their lack of trust.

Jesus was perturbed. So, Jesus did something that is described so beautifully by Saint John in just three little words: *And Jesus wept.*

"... that they may believe that you sent me... Lazarus, come out."

Today's Gospel reading is painted on the back wall of our Church, and in our painting you can see Lazarus being called out by Jesus. Mary and Martha are present in the painting, as well.

One of our other stained glass windows depicts the Resurrection of our Lord and Savior Jesus Christ. It is found on the East wall of our Church. Do not compare the two events. They have nothing in common. Why?

Because Lazarus died again.

Martha died... and Mary died... and the crowd of Jews assembled in Bethany on that day died, as well. What Lazarus received in today's Gospel reading was a reprieve from death.

Let me return to something I touched on earlier. Today's Gospel reading is the Gospel according to Saint John. It is Sacrament.

The life of the Risen Christ cannot die again. So, where is the life of the Risen Christ found, today?

The Risen Christ is seated at the right hand of the Father. The Risen Christ lives in the Holy Eucharist. And the Risen Christ lives within you and me. We received the life of the Risen Christ at canon. The life of the Risen Christ is with us forever in Baptism.

You and I have another name, other than the one bestowed upon us during our baptism. Our other name is: Lazarus. Today's Gospel reading is about the Sacraments. It is about the Church. It is about us.

My favorite author is Caryl Houselander, and in her little book, the one that I have spoken of a million times, *The Reed of God*, Caryl explains that Jesus used all manner of things to bring people closer to God. He used water that became wine. He multiplied bread. He used saliva and earth to open eyes. But Houselander wrote that the greatest material Jesus ever used was Lazarus, because it was dead.

Because it was dead.

Sometimes the life of Christ that lives within you and lives within me gets weak. Sometimes it appears to die. To us it seems to die because of something in our lives we really do not like to talk about... it is called sin. And sin is very real.

There are times when each of us is like Lazarus... the dead Lazarus. Sometimes we feel dead inside. Sometimes we feel our faith has gone. Sometimes we feel we cannot pray or that prayer is of little use to us. Sometimes we become trapped in our sinful habits. Sometimes we feel covered by the earth. And when we feel like that... there is Jesus... who takes His own time... but who comes with the power of His Father.

And when it seems that everyone else is ready to give up on us... when we are ready to give up on ourselves... outside the tomb of our fear and the tomb of our despair stands Jesus. He calls to you and He calls to me through the Sacrament of Reconciliation and through the Sacrament of the Eucharist, to be who we were at Baptism. He cries out to each of, *"Lazarus, come out!"*

My favorite line in today's Gospel reading is the last one spoken by Jesus to Mary, and to Martha, and to the crowd of Jews assembled at the entrance of Lazarus' tomb.

"Untie him and let him go."

Fr. Lavalley

We acknowledge one baptism for the forgiveness of sins...

Palm Sunday of the Lord's Passion

A reading from the Book of the Prophet Isaiah:

The Lord God has given me a well-trained tongue, that I might know how to speak to the weary a word that will rouse them. Morning after morning he opens my ear that I may hear; and I have not rebelled, have not turned back. I gave my back to those who beat me, my cheeks to those who plucked my beard; my face I did not shield from buffets and spitting.

The Lord God is my help, therefore I am not disgraced; I have set my face like flint, knowing that I shall not be put to shame.

A reading from the Letter of Saint Paul to the Philippians:

Christ Jesus, though he was in the form of God, did not regard equality with God something to be grasped. Rather, he emptied himself, taking the form of a slave, coming in human likeness; and found human in appearance, he humbled himself, becoming obedient to the point of death, even death on a cross. Because of this, God greatly exalted him and bestowed on him the name which is above every name, that at the name of Jesus every knee should bend, of those in heaven and on earth and under the earth, and every tongue confess that Jesus Christ is Lord, to the glory of God the Father.

The Passion of the Lord according to Saint Matthew:

One of the twelve, who was called Judas Iscariot, went to the chief priests and said, "What are you willing to give me if I hand him over to you?"

They paid him thirty pieces of silver, and from that time on he looked for an opportunity to hand him over.

On the first day of the Feast of Unleavened Bread, the disciples approached Jesus and said, "Where do you want us to prepare for you to eat the Passover?"

He said, "Go into the city to a certain man and tell him, 'The teacher says, "My appointed time draws near; in your house I shall celebrate the Passover with my disciples."'"

The disciples then did as Jesus had ordered, and prepared the Passover.

When it was evening, he reclined at table with the Twelve. And while they were eating he said, "Amen, I say to you, one of you will betray me."

Deeply distressed at this, they began to say to him one after another, "Surely it is not I, Lord?"

He said in reply, "He who has dipped his hand into the dish with me is the one who will betray me. The Son of Man indeed goes, as it is written of him, but woe to that man by whom the Son of Man is betrayed. It would be better for that man if he had never been born."

Then Judas, his betrayer, said in reply, "Surely it is not I, Rabbi?"

He answered, "You have said so."

While they were eating, Jesus took bread, said the blessing, broke it, and giving it to his disciples said, "Take and eat; this is my body."

Then he took a cup, gave thanks, and gave it to them, saying, "Drink from it, all of you, for this is my blood of the covenant, which will be shed on behalf of the many for the forgiveness of sins. I tell you, from now on I shall not drink this fruit of the vine until the day when I drink it with you new in the kingdom of my Father."

Then, after singing a hymn, they went out to the Mount of Olives.

Then Jesus said to them, "This night all of you will have your faith in me shaken, for it is written: I will strike the shepherd, and the sheep of the flock will be dispersed. But after I have been raised up, I shall go before you to Galilee."

Peter said to him in reply, "Though all may have their faith in you shaken, mine will never be."

Jesus said to him, "Amen, I say to you, this very night before the cock crows, you will deny me three times."

Peter said to him, "Even though I should have to die with you, I will not deny you."

And all the disciples spoke likewise.

Then Jesus came with them to a place called Gethsemane, and he said to his disciples, "Sit here while I go over there and pray."

He took along Peter and the two sons of Zebedee, and began to feel sorrow and distress. Then he said to them, "My soul is sorrowful even to death. Remain here and keep watch with me."

He advanced a little and fell prostrate in prayer, saying, "My Father, if it is possible, let this cup pass from me; yet, not as I will, but as you will."

When he returned to his disciples he found them asleep. He said to Peter, "So you could not keep watch with me for one hour? Watch and pray that you may not undergo the test. The spirit is willing, but the flesh is weak."

Withdrawing a second time, he prayed again, "My Father, if it is not possible that this cup pass without my drinking it, your will be done!"

Then he returned once more and found them asleep. For they could not keep their eyes open. He left them and withdrew again and prayed a third time saying the same thing again. Then he returned to his disciples and said to them, "Are you sleeping and taking your rest? Behold, the hour is at hand when the Son of Man is to be handed over to sinners. Get up, let us go. Look my betrayer is at hand."

While he was still speaking, Judas, one of the Twelve, arrived, accompanied by a large crowd, with swords and clubs, who had come from the chief priests and elders of the people. His betrayer had arranged a sign with them, saying, "The man I shall kiss is the one; arrest him."

Immediately he went over to Jesus and said, "Hail, Rabbi!" And he kissed him.

Jesus answered him, "Friend, do what you have come for."

Then stepping forward they laid hands on Jesus and arrested him. And behold, one of those who accompanied Jesus put his hand to his sword, drew it, and struck the high priest's servant, cutting off his ear. Then Jesus said to him, "Put your sword back into its sheath, for all those who take the sword will perish by the sword. Do you think that I cannot call upon my Father and he will not provide me at this moment with more than twelve legions of angels? But then how would the Scriptures be fulfilled which say that it must come to pass in this way?"

At that hour Jesus said to the crowds, "Have you come out as against a robber, with clubs and sword to seize me? Day after day I sat teaching in the temple area, yet you did not arrest me. But all this has come to pass that the writings of the prophets may be fulfilled."

Then all the disciples left him and fled.

Those who had arrested Jesus led him away to Caiaphas the high priest, where the scribes and the elders were assembled. Peter was following him at a distance as far as the high priests courtyard, and going inside he sat down with the servants to see the outcome. The chief priests and the entire Sanhedrin kept trying to obtain false testimony against Jesus in order to put him to death, but they found none, though many false witnesses came forward. Finally two came forward who stated, "This man said, 'I can destroy the temple of God and within three days rebuild it.'"

The high priest rose and addressed him, "Have you no answer? What are these men testifying against you?"

But Jesus was silent. Then the high priest said to him, "I order you to tell us under oath before the living God whether you are the Christ, the Son of God."

Jesus said to him in reply, "You have said so. But I tell you: From now on you will see 'the Son of Man seated at the right hand of the Power' and 'coming on the clouds of heaven.'"

Then the high priest tore his robes and said, "He has blasphemed! What further need have we of witnesses? You have heard the blasphemy; what is your opinion?"

They said in reply, "He deserves to die!"

Then they spat in his face and struck him, while some slapped him, saying, "Prophesy for us, Christ: who is that struck you?"

Now Peter was sitting outside in the courtyard. One of the maids came over to him and said, "You were with Jesus the Galilean."

But he denied it in front of everyone, saying, "I do not know what you are talking about!"

As he went out to the gate, another girl saw him and said to those who were there, "This man was with Jesus of Nazareth."

Again he denied it with an oath, "I do not know the man!"

A little later the bystanders came over and said to Peter, "Surely you too are one of them; even your speech gives you away."

At that time he began to curse and to swear, "I do not know the man."

And immediately a cock crowed. Then Peter remembered the word that Jesus had spoken: "Before the cock crows you will deny me three times." He went out and began to weep bitterly.

When it was morning, all the chief priests and elders of the people took counsel against Jesus to put him to death. They bound him, led him away, and handed him over to Pilate, the governor. Then Judas, his betrayer, seeing that Jesus had been condemned deeply regretted what he had done. He returned the thirty pieces of silver to the chief priests and elders, saying, "I have sinned in betraying innocent blood."

They said, "What is that to us? Look to it yourself."

Flinging the money into the temple, he departed and went off and hanged himself. The chief priests gathered up the money but said, "It is not lawful to deposit this in the temple treasury, for it is the price of blood."

After consultation, they used it to buy the potter's field as a burial place for foreigners. That is why even to day it is called the Field of Blood.

Then was fulfilled what had been said through Jeremiah the prophet, "And they took the thirty pieces of silver, the value of a man with a price on his head, a price set by some of the Israelites, and they paid it out for the potter's field just as the Lord had commanded me."

Now, Jesus stood before the governor, Pontius Pilate, and he questioned him, "Are you the king of the Jews?"

Jesus said, "You say so."

And when he was accused by the chief priests and elders, he made no answer. Then Pilate said to him, "Do you not hear how many things they are testifying against you?"

But he did not answer one word so that the governor was greatly amazed.

Now on the occasion of the feast of the governor was accustomed to release to the crowd one prisoner whom they wished. And at that time they had a notorious prisoner called Barabbas. So when they had assembled, Pilate said to them, "Which one do you want me to release to you, Barabbas, or Jesus called Christ?"

For he knew that it was out of envy that they had handed him over. While he was seated on the bench, his wife sent him a message, "Have nothing to do with that righteous man. I suffered much in a dream today because of him." The chief priests and the elders persuaded the crowds to ask for Barabbas but to destroy Jesus. The governor said to them in reply, "Which of the two do you want me to release to you?"

They answered, "Barabbas!"

Pilate said to them, "Then what shall I do with Jesus called Christ?"

They all said, "Let him be crucified!"

But he said, "Why? What evil has he done?"

They only shouted the louder, "Let him be crucified!"

When Pilate saw that he was not succeeding at all, but that a riot was breaking out instead, he took water and washed his hands in the sight of the crowd, saying, "I am innocent of this man's blood. Look to it yourselves."

And the whole people said in reply, "His blood be upon us and upon our children."

Then he released Barabbas to them, but after he had Jesus scourged, he handed him over to be crucified.

Then the soldiers of the governor took Jesus inside the praetorium and gathered the whole cohort around him. They stripped him of his clothes and threw a scarlet military cloak about him. Weaving a crown out of thorns, they placed it on his head, and a reed in his right hand. And kneeling before him, they mocked him, saying, "Hail, King of the Jews!"

They spat upon him and took the reed and kept striking him on the head. And when they had mocked him, they stripped him of the cloak, dressed him in his own clothes, and led him off to crucify him.

As they were going out, they met a Cyrenian named Simon; this man they pressed into service to carry his cross. And when they came to a place called Golgotha, which means Place of the Skull, they gave Jesus wine to drink mixed with gall. But when he had tasted it, he refused to drink. After they had crucified him, they divided his garments by casting lots; then they sat down and kept watch over him there. And they placed over his head the written charge against him: "This is Jesus, the King of the Jews." Two revolutionaries were crucified with him, one on his right and the other on his left. Those passing by reviled him, shaking their heads and saying, "You who would destroy the temple and rebuild it in three days, save yourself, if you are the Son of God, and come down from the cross!"

Likewise the chief priests with the scribes and elders mocked him and said, "He saved others; he cannot save himself. So he is the king of Israel! Let him come down from the cross now and we will believe in him. He trusted God; let Him deliver him now if He wants him. For he said, 'I am the Son of God.'"

The revolutionaries who were crucified with him also kept abusing him in the same way.

From noon onward, darkness came over the whole land until three in the afternoon. And about three o'clock Jesus cried out in a loud voice, "Eli, Eli, lema sabachthani?" Which means, "My God, my God, why have you forsaken me?"

Some of the bystanders who heard it said, "This one is calling for Elijah."

Immediately one of them ran to get a sponge; he soaked it in wine, and putting it on a reed, gave it to him to drink. But the rest said, "Wait, let us see if Elijah comes to save him."

But Jesus cried out again in a loud voice, and gave up his spirit.

And behold, the veil of the sanctuary was torn in two from top to bottom. The earth quaked, rocks were split, tombs were opened, and the bodies of many saints who had fallen asleep were raised. And coming forth from their tombs after his resurrection, they entered the holy city and appeared to many. The centurion and the men with him who were keeping watch over Jesus feared greatly when they saw the earthquake and all that was happening, and they said, "Truly, this was the Son of God!"

There were many women there, looking on from a distance, who had followed Jesus from Galilee, ministering to him. Among them were Mary Magdalene and Mary the mother of James and Joseph, and the mother of the sons of Zebedee. When it was evening, there came a rich *man from Arimathea named Joseph, who himself was a disciple of Jesus. He went to Pilate and asked for the body of Jesus; then Pilate ordered it to be handed over. Taking the body, Joseph wrapped it in clean linen and laid it in his new tomb that he had hewn in the rock. Then he rolled a huge stone across the entrance to the tomb and departed. But Mary Magdalene and the other Mary remained sitting there, facing the tomb.*

The next day, the one following the day of preparation, the chief priests and the Pharisees gathered before Pilate and said, "Sir, we remember that this imposter while still alive said, 'After three days I will be raised up.' Give orders then that the grave be secured until the third day, lest his disciples come and steal him and say to the people, 'He has been raised from the dead.' This last imposture would be worse than the first."

Pilate said to them, "The guard is yours; go, secure it as best you can."

So they went and secured the tomb by fixing a seal to the stone and setting the guard.

The reading of the Passion, in and of itself, is the Palm Sunday homily, but let us focus for a few short minutes on the things we need to carry away from here with us.

Passion is an interesting word. Especially when we use it to describe the suffering and death of the God man. We refer to the suffering and the death of Jesus Christ as: His Passion. What is passion?

Passion is something that runs very deep within us.

We say, "She is a passionate painter. He has a passion for justice. We love someone, passionately. Singing was her great passion."

We know what passion means... do we not?

Passion means the center of someone's focus... the whole of their life's energy.

The center and the focus of Jesus' life is... us. We are His passion.

It was all done for us. All of it.

Let us take a brief look at some of the characters in today's Gospel reading. The one who always sticks out right away is Judas, is it not?

What did Jesus call Judas in today's Gospel reading?

In the moment of his betrayal, what did Jesus call Judas?

Friend.

That was not sarcasm on the part of Jesus. That was love.

Friend.

How about Peter?

Jesus loved Peter.

How about the crowd?

Jesus loved the crowd.

We learn something very important about the heart of Jesus, especially when we compare it to the human heart.

During our Palm Sunday procession to the altar in the length of an aisle we went from singing *"Hosanna, blessed is he who comes in the name of the Lord"* to the reading of the Passion and cries of *"Crucify Him."* All of this in a matter of minutes.

Despite all that was wrought upon Him, Jesus remains passionate in His love for us.

Gaius Cassius Longinus is the name given to the centurion who pierced the side of Jesus with a spear. And for putting his spear into the side of Jesus, what was Gaius Cassius given?

He was given the gift of faith.

My Lord... my God... that was his revelation.

The first canonization the Church had ever known was not done by a Pope, it was by Jesus, Himself, and it was on the Cross and He canonized a thief. *"Truly, I say to you, today you will be with me in Paradise."*

Archbishop Sheen wrote, "And the good thief died a thief. He died stealing heaven, and heaven can be stolen again."

Jesus loved them all.

The problem with everyone of them was that they did not and could not see who He was. Jesus made that excuse for them even to the very end when He said, *"Father, forgive them for they know not what they do."*

They did not know what they were doing. They saw everything, but the Son of God. Their sin was blindness.

Today, that same Jesus loves you and that same Jesus loves me. And if all of this is to mean anything... anything at all... it cannot simply be tears and wailing. We must have the vision of the Son of God.

Prejudice... any kind at all... hatred... revenge... the lack of forgiveness... we simply cannot permit those things to enter our hearts and guide our lives.

If we take away anything from the Passion of the Christ let it be, *"Love one another as I have loved you."*

Fr. Lavalley

We look for the resurrection of the dead...

Holy Thursday,
Evening of the Lord's Supper

A reading from the Book of Exodus:

The Lord said to Moses and Aaron in the land of Egypt, "This month shall stand at the head of your calendar; you shall reckon it the first month of the year. Tell the whole community of Israel: On the tenth of this month every one of your families must procure for itself a lamb, one apiece for each household. If a family is too small for a whole lamb, it shall join the nearest household in procuring one and shall share in the lamb in proportion to the number of persons who partake of it. The lamb must be without blemish. You may take it from either the sheep or the goats. You shall keep it until the fourteenth day of this month, and then, with the whole assembly of Israel present, it shall be slaughtered during the evening twilight. They shall take some of its blood and apply it to the two doorposts and the lintel of every house in which they partake of the lamb. That same night they shall eat its roasted flesh with unleavened bread and bitter herbs."

"This is how you are to eat it: with your loins girt, sandals on your feet and your staff in hand, you shall eat like those who are in flight. It is the Passover of the Lord. For on this same night I will go through Egypt, striking down every firstborn of the land, both man and beast, and

executing judgment on all the gods of Egypt- I, the Lord! But the blood will mark the houses where you are. Seeing the blood, I will pass over you; thus, when I strike the land of Egypt, no destructive blow will come upon you."

"This day shall be a memorial feast for you, which all your generations shall celebrate with pilgrimage to the Lord, as a perpetual institution."

A reading from the first Letter of Saint Paul to the Corinthians:

Brothers and sisters: I received from the Lord what I also handed on to you, that the Lord Jesus, on the night he was handed over, took bread, and after he had given thanks, broke it and said, "This is my body that is for you. Do this in remembrance of me." In the same way also the cup, after supper saying, "This cup is the new covenant in my blood. Do this, as often as you drink it, in remembrance of me." For as often as you eat this bread and drink the cup, you will proclaim the death of the Lord until he comes.

A reading from the holy Gospel according to John:

Before the feast of Passover, Jesus knew that his hour had come to pass from this world to the Father. He loved his own in the world and he loved them to the end. The devil had already induced Judas, son of Simon the Iscariot, to hand him over. So, during supper, fully aware that the Father had put everything into his power and that he had come from God and was returning to God, he rose from supper and took off his outer garments. He took a towel and tied it around his waist. Then he poured water into a basin and began to wash the disciples' feet and dry them with the towel around his waist. He came to Simon Peter, who said to him, "Master, are you going to wash my feet?" Jesus answered and said to him, "What I am doing now, you do not understand now, but you will understand later." Peter said to him, "You will never wash my feet."

Jesus answered him, "Unless I wash you, you will have no inheritance with me." Simon Peter said to him, "Master, then not only my feet, but my hands and head as well." Jesus said to him, "Whoever has bathed has no need except to have his feet washed, for he is clean all over; so you are clean, but not all." For he knew who would betray him; for this reason, he said, "Not all of you are clean."

So when he washed their feet and put his garments back on and reclined at table again, he said to them, "Do you realize what I have done for you? You call me 'teacher' and 'master,' and rightly so, for indeed I am. If I, therefore, the master and teacher, have washed your feet, you ought to wash another's feet. I have given you a model to follow, so that as I have done for you, you should also do."

The Holy Days of Obligation are all wonderful days, but I absolutely love Holy Thursday.

There is a wonderful old movie called *The Shoes of the Fisherman*, by Morris West. It is a marvelous movie. And while I will not retell the whole tale here, I will describe one of its scenes to you.

In this one particular scene a woman is speaking with a pope. However, she does not know that the man with whom she is speaking is a pope. She is speaking with him about bitterness in her heart and troubles in her relationships. She is describing for him how awful things have turned out for her in her life. During the course of her conversation with the pope, she begins to suspect whom he is. She asks, "What would the man in the white cassock say?"

The Pope replies, "Oh, the man in the white cassock would have to call a congress. He would have to convene a council. He would have to consult with many people before he could reply... but the heart of the man inside of the white cassock would say, 'Of all the things you have spoken, you have never once mentioned love.' Was there ever any love?"

The woman says, "Oh yes... there was love; once upon a time."

The Pope responds by saying, "Ah... If there was love, there still is love. You have simply misplaced it. Try to recall where it was you last saw love. Remember... and you will find it again."

Saint Francis Xavier, our church, is filled with sacred space. Where the Baptismal Fount is... that is sacred space. Where our deacons sit in the Sanctuary... that is sacred space. Where I sit behind the Altar... that is sacred space. The Pulpit, where I stand to speak with you... that is sacred space. Where the Eucharist resides in the Tabernacle... that is very sacred space. But let me point out other sacred space to you... sacred space you probably did not know existed.

Where you sit... the pews within which you sit when we come together as a parish in celebration of our love for Jesus Christ, that is sacred space. And, within each and everyone one of you... that is sacred space.

Where you are and who you are is sacred space because it contains the holiest of holiness. You are sacred space because you hold the Body of Christ that comes together in sacrament and sign on this Holy Thursday; to celebrate what we do every day when we come together; to accept the Holy Eucharist; to become the Holy Eucharist. You are sacred and holy space.

Yes... we are broken. And yes... we are sinful. But yes... we belong to God. And He loves us.

God wants our brokenness, our dirty feet, our dirty souls, and that little Iscariot that lives inside each and everyone of us.

He wants us to make it holy.

The Eucharist exists for us.

"Recall where it was you last saw love..."

This day I am going to ask you to take a journey with me. I would like to take you on a journey way back in time to the day of your first Holy Communion. I want you to remember your first Holy Communion as best you can.

Do you remember how you prepared for your first Holy Communion?

Do you remember what you were taught?

I recall being taught that I had to be very, very good, because I was going to receive Jesus Christ within me. And I prepared for that moment with the Sacrament of Confession. I tried so hard not to do anything that would make me unworthy to receive Jesus Christ in the Holy Eucharist.

Do you remember the thrill of your first Holy Communion?

It is easy to forget, is it not?

I invite you to take a look at your own history with the Holy Eucharist. Sometimes we slip away. Sometimes we come back again.

Holy Thursday... let us take this opportunity to make our first Holy Communion, again. *Unless you turn and become like children, you will never enter the Kingdom of Heaven.*

Let us prepare for it right now.

We need to speak with Jesus. We need to tell Him we are sorry that we sometimes forget what a wonderful gift it is to receive Him through the Holy Eucharist. We need to tell Him we are sorry for the times we take the Holy Eucharist for granted... and while swallowing the Host, we are thinking of everything else, but Jesus Christ.

Holy Thursday calls us to fall in love with Jesus, all over again.

It is interesting that the Gospel reading for Holy Thursday is not the institution narrative of the Holy Eucharist. Did you notice that today's Gospel reading reflects what comes before receiving the Holy Eucharist. It speaks to the condition for the Holy Eucharist. It speaks of washing feet.

Nowadays we symbolically wash feet, but each and every one of us has people we need to forgive. Look at the crowd of people whose feet Jesus washed. Every single one of them, with the exception of John, is going to leave Him... is going to disavow knowing Him on the morning of Good Friday. Jesus knows this, yet, He still washes their feet...

Jesus' love is pure and knows no limits.

When we receive the Holy Eucharist, we need to bring our people to the altar with us... the ones whom we find hardest to love. We need to pray for those with whom we do not get along. We need to pray for those who have offended us, those who have hurt us. It is a condition set forth for receiving the Holy Eucharist.

Being able to forgive is such an important condition. Being ready to forgive is so much more important than any other pious feelings we may possess. Pious feelings are good, but the Holy Eucharist challenges us to be the Holy Eucharist... to kneel at the feet of Judas... to wash the feet of Judas.

We need to be who we receive... Jesus Christ.

If there are parts of our lives, right now, that are broken and fragmented, and wounded and hurt... if there is a part of our human heart that is turned to ice... we need to go to Jesus. Let Him wash your feet. Let Him in. Do not be like Peter who said, "I cannot let you do it."

Let Him do it.

If the only thing God wants of us is our self... it is not the fault self. The fault self does not exist. It is not the ideal self. The ideal self does not exist. And it is not the saint that you and I want to be... or say we want to be. It is only you.

What an exchange. I get Jesus, and Jesus gets...

Me...

Fr. Lavalley

Good Friday of the Lord's Passion

A reading from the Book of the Prophet Isaiah:

See, my servant shall prosper, he shall be raised high and greatly exalted. Even as many were amazed at him, so marred was his look beyond human semblance and his appearance beyond that of the sons of man, so shall he startle many nations, because of him kings shall stand speechless; for those who have not been told shall see, those who have not heard shall ponder it.

Who would believe what we have heard? To whom has the arm of the Lord been revealed?

He grew up like a sapling before him, like a shoot from the parched earth; there was in him no stately bearing to make us look at him, nor appearance that would attract us to him. He was spurned and avoided by people, a man of suffering, accustomed to infirmity, one of those from whom people hide their faces, spurned, and we held in him no esteem.

Yet it was our infirmities that he bore, our sufferings that he endured, while we thought of him as stricken, as one smitten by God and afflicted. But he was pierced for our offenses, crushed for our sins; upon him was the chastisement that makes us whole, by his stripes we were healed. We had all gone astray like sheep, each following his own way; but the Lord laid upon him the guilt of us all.

Though he was harshly treated, he submitted and opened not his mouth; like a lamb led to the slaughter or a sheep before the shearers, he was silent and opened not his mouth. Oppressed and condemned, he was taken away, and who would have thought any more of his destiny? When he was cut off from the land of the living, and smitten for the sin of his people, a grave was assigned him among the wicked and a burial place with the evildoers, though he had done no wrong nor spoken any falsehoods. But the Lord was pleased to crush him in infirmity.

If he gives his life as an offering for sin, he shall see his descendants in a long life, and the will of the Lord shall be accomplished through him.

Because of his affliction he shall see the light in the fullness of days; through his suffering, my servant shall justify many, and their guilt he shall bear. Therefore I will give him his portion among the great, and he shall divide the spoils with the mighty, because he surrendered himself to death and was counted among the wicked; and he shall take away the sins of the many and win pardon for their offenses.

A reading from the Letter to the Hebrews:

Brothers and sisters: Since we have a great high priest who has passed through the heavens, Jesus, the Son of God, let us hold fast to our confession. For we do not have a high priest who is unable to sympathize with our weaknesses, but one who has similarly been tested in every way, yet without sin. So let us confidently approach the throne of grace to receive mercy and to find grace for timely help.

In the days when Christ was in the flesh, he offered prayers and supplications with loud cries and tears to the one who was able to save him from death, and he was heard because of his reverence. Son though he was, he learned obedience from what he suffered; and when he was made perfect, he became the source of eternal salvation for all who obey him.

The Passion of our Lord according to Saint John:

Jesus went out with his disciples across the Kidron valley to where there was a garden, into which he and his disciples entered. Judas his betrayer also knew the place, because Jesus had often met there with his disciples. So Judas got a band of soldiers and guards from the chief priests and the Pharisees and went there with lanterns, torches, and weapons. Jesus, knowing everything that was going to happen to him, went out and said to them, "Whom are you looking for?"

They answered him, "Jesus of Nazareth."

He said to them, "I AM."

Judas his betrayer was also with them. When he said to them, "I AM," they turned away and fell to the ground. So he again asked them, "Whom are you looking for?"

They said, "Jesus the Nazorean."

Jesus answered, "I told you that I AM. So if you are looking for me, let these men go."

This was to fulfill what he had said, "I have not lost any of those you gave me." Then Simon Peter, who had a sword, drew it, struck the high priest's slave, and cut off his right ear. The slave's name was Malchus. Jesus said to Peter, "Put your sword into its scabbard. Shall I not drink the cup that the Father gave me?"

So the band of soldiers, the tribune, and the Jewish guards seized Jesus, bound him, and brought him to Annas first. He was the father-in-law of Caiaphas, who was the high priest that year. It was Caiaphas who had counseled the Jews that it was better that one man should die rather than the people. Simon Peter and another disciple followed Jesus. Now the other disciple was known to the high priest, and he entered the courtyard of the high priest with Jesus. But Peter stood at the gate outside. So the other disciple, the acquaintance of the high priest, went out and spoke to the gatekeeper and brought Peter in. The maid who was the gatekeeper said to Peter, "You are not one of this man's disciples, are you?"

He said, "I am not."

Now the slaves and the guards who were standing around a charcoal fire that they had made, because it was cold, and were warming themselves. Peter was also standing there keeping warm.

The high priest questioned Jesus about his disciples and about his doctrine. Jesus answered him, "I have spoken publicly to the world. I have always taught in a synagogue or in the temple area where all the Jews gather, and in secret I have said nothing. Why ask me? Ask those who heard me what I said to them. They know what I said."

When he had said this, one of the temple guards standing there struck Jesus and said, "Is this the way you answer the high priest?"

Jesus answered him, "If I have spoken wrongly, testify to the wrong; but if I have spoken rightly, why do you strike me?"

Then Annas sent him bound to Caiaphas the high priest.

Now Simon Peter was standing there keeping warm. And they said to him, "You are not one of his disciples, are you?"

He denied it and said, "I am not."

One of the slaves of the high priest, a relative of the one whose ear Peter had cut off, said, "Didn't I see you in the garden with him?"

Again Peter denied it. And immediately the cock crowed.

Then they brought Jesus from Caiaphas to the praetorium. It was morning. And they themselves did not enter the praetorium, in order not to be defiled so that they could eat the Passover. So Pilate came out to them and said, "What charge do you bring against this man?"

They answered and said to him, "If he were not a criminal, we would not have handed him over to you."

At this, Pilate said to them, "Take him yourselves, and judge him according to your law."

The Jews answered him, "We do not have the right to execute anyone." This was to fulfill the word that Jesus had spoken to show by what kind of death he was going to die.

So Pilate went back into the praetorium and summoned Jesus and said to him, "Are you the King of the Jews?"

Jesus answered, "Do you say this on your own or have others told you about me?"

Pilate answered, "I am not a Jew, am I? Your own nation and the chief priests handed you over to me. What have you done?"

Jesus answered, "My kingdom does not belong to this world. If my kingdom did belong to this world, my attendants would be fighting to keep me from being handed over to the Jews. But as it is, my kingdom is not here."

So Pilate said to him, "Then you are a king?"

Jesus answered, "You say I am a king. For this I was born and for this I came into this world, to testify to the truth. Everyone who belongs to the truth listens to my voice."

Pilate said to him, "What is truth?"

When he had said this, he again went out to the Jews and said to them, "I find no guilt in him. But you have a custom that I release one prisoner to you at Passover. Do you want me to release to you the King of the Jews?"

They cried out again, "Not this one but Barabbas!"

Now Barabbas was a revolutionary.

Then Pilate took Jesus and had him scourged. And the soldiers wove a crown out of thorns and placed it on his head, and clothed him in a purple cloak, and they came to him and said, "Hail, King of the Jews!"

And they struck him repeatedly. Once more Pilate went out and said to them, "look, I am bringing him out to you so that you may know that I find no guilt in him."

So Jesus came out, wearing the crown of thorns and the purple cloak. And Pilate said to them, "Behold, the man!"

When the chief priests and the guards saw him they cried out, "Crucify him, crucify him!"

Pilate said to them, "Take him yourselves and crucify him. I find no guilt in him."

The Jews answered, "We have a law, and according to the law he ought to die, because he made himself the Son of God."

Now when Pilate heard this statement he became even more afraid, and went back into the praetorium and said to Jesus, "Where are you from?"

Jesus did not answer him. So Pilate said to him, "Do you not speak to me? Do you not know that I have power to release you and I have power to crucify you?"

Jesus answered him, "You would have no power over me if it had not been given to you from above. For this reason the one who handed me over to you has the greater sin."

Consequently, Pilate tried to release him, but the Jews cried out, "If you release him, you are not a friend of Caesar. Everyone who makes himself a king opposes Caesar."

When Pilate heard these words he brought Jesus out and seated him on the judge's bench in the place called Stone Pavement, in Hebrew, Gabbatha. It was preparation day for Passover, and it was about noon. And he said to the Jews, Behold, your king!"

They cried out, "Take him away, take him away! Crucify him!"

Pilate said to them, "Shall I crucify your king?"

The chief priests answered, "We have no king but Caesar."

Then he handed him over to them to be crucified.

So they took Jesus, and, carrying the cross himself, he went out to what is called the Place of the Skull, in Hebrew, Golgotha. There they crucified him, and with two others, one on either side, with Jesus in the middle. Pilate also had an inscription written and put on the cross. It read, "Jesus the Nazorean, the King of the Jews." Now many of the Jews read this inscription, because the place where Jesus was crucified was near the city; and it was written in Hebrew, Latin, and Greek. So the chief priests of the Jews said to Pilate, "Do not write 'The King of the Jews,' but that he said, 'I am the King of the Jews.'"

Pilate answered, "What I have written, I have written."

When the soldiers had crucified Jesus, they took his clothes and divided them into four shares, a share for each soldier. They also took his tunic, but the tunic was seamless, woven in one piece from the top down.

So they said to one another, "Let's not tear it, but cast lots for it to see whose it will be," in order that the passage of Scripture might be fulfilled that says: "They divided my garments among them, and for my vesture they cast lots."

This is what the soldiers did. Standing by the cross of Jesus were his mother and his mother's sister, Mary the wife of Clopas, and Mary of Magdala. When Jesus saw his mother and the disciple there whom he loved he said to his mother, "Woman, behold, your son."

Then he said to the disciple, "Behold, your mother." And from that hour the disciple took her into his home.

After this, aware that everything was now finished, in order that the Scripture might be fulfilled, Jesus said, "I thirst."

There was a vessel filled with common wine. So they put a sponge soaked in wine on a sprig of hyssop and put it up to his mouth. When Jesus had taken the wine, he said, "It is finished." And bowing his head, he handed over the spirit.

Now since it was preparation day, in order that the bodies might not remain on the cross on the Sabbath, for the Sabbath day of that week was a solemn one, the Jews asked Pilate that their legs be broken and that they be taken down. So the soldiers came and broke the legs of the first and then the other one who was crucified with Jesus. But when they came to Jesus and saw that he was already dead, they did not break his legs, but one soldier thrust his lance into his side, and immediately blood and water flowed out. An eyewitness has testified, and his testimony is true; he knows that he is speaking the truth, so that you also may come to believe. For this happened so that the Scripture passage might by fulfilled: "Not a bone of it will be broken." And again another passage says, "They will look upon him whom they have pierced."

After this, Joseph of Arimathea, secretly a disciple of Jesus for fear of the Jews, asked Pilate if he could remove the body of Jesus. And Pilate permitted it. So he came and took his body. Nicodemus, the one who had first come to him at night, also came bringing a mixture of myrrh and aloes weighing about one hundred pounds. They took the body of Jesus and bound it with burial cloths along with the spices, according to the Jewish burial custom. Now in the place where he had been crucified there was a garden, and in the garden a new tomb, in which no one had yet been buried. So they laid Jesus there because of the Jewish preparation day; for the tomb was close by.

We need to dig deep. We need to dig very deep... because, if we do not, we might end up simply looking at a broken body: a body scourged; a head crowned with thorns; and a man crucified. And if we are not careful, our whole attention will be focused on His wounds and not the reality at what we need to look and the reality of where we need to look.

We must never forget who Jesus was... who Jesus is... and who Jesus will always be.

In the manifestation of Jesus Christ, our charge is to reconcile our human experience with something that is called the Hypostatic Union: a fifty cent phrase describing something very beautiful and supremely mysterious.

For God so loved the world that he gave His only begotten Son.

There are two natures to Jesus Christ. He is truly God... and He is truly man. He is truly one of us. It is the unique summit of God's creative power: blending His own nature with our human nature. But if we are to understand the mystery of Good Friday, we need to keep our minds focused on the person of Jesus.

The person of Jesus is... God.

Jesus is co-eternal with the Father. Always was... always will be. A Father who loved us so much that He took on our flesh to save us from our sin.

If we concentrated solely on His wounds, it would be ridiculous to call this day "Good Friday."

We do not call this day "Horrible Friday" or "Bad Friday" or "Suffering Friday." Lovingly, the Church has always called this day "Good Friday" because, ultimately, this day is a story of love. It is a story of a love that conquers death, and a love that conquers sin. And the secret to this day exists in the first lines of today's Gospel. Those words are the ones we need to consider.

What was the question Jesus asked of the band of soldiers and guards sent by the chief priests and the Pharisees to arrest Him?

"Whom do you seek?"

This very question is asked of you, today. It is asked of this diocese, this country, and this world.

"Whom do you seek?"

This very question is asked from the pulpit of our holy father in Rome, and of the newest baby baptized in our church. It is a question for all of us.

"Whom do you seek?"

In today's Gospel, the soldiers and the guards replied, *"Jesus of Nazareth."*

Jesus' answer to them is so powerful, because it goes back to the person of Jesus. He is not simply the son of Mary and the carpenter, Joseph. There is so much more than the humanity of Jesus speaking to us. It is a memory triggered.

What is the answer?

It sprang from a past long departed. The answer was simply, *"I AM."*

I AM.

Not, "I am Jesus."

Not, "I am the carpenter's son."

Not, "I am Jesus of Nazareth."

Two words: *I AM.*

Do you know that answer?

Have you ever heard that response before this Scripture reading?

Yes... you have!

Thousand of years before the Gospel according to Saint John was scribed, another man climbed another mountain. He was chosen to lead his people into the first exodus. His name was Moses, and the angel of the Lord appeared to him in a flame of fire out of the midst of a bush. And when the hidden God in the burning bush bestowed upon Moses the responsibility of bringing God's people, the children of Israel, out of Egypt, Moses asked, *"If I come to the people of Israel and say to them, 'The God of your fathers has sent me to you,' and they ask me, 'What is his name?' what shall I say to them?"*

From that burning bush the Hebrew God, hidden from Moses by flame, replied, and He said, *"I AM WHO I AM."*

"Say this to the people of Israel, 'I AM has sent me to you.'"

"Whom do you seek in the garden?"

"Jesus of Nazareth."

I AM.

Jesus touches the very core of His divinity... identifying with the Father.

There was a wonderful artist, who worked with all kinds of materials. His name was Ferdinand Pie. He created beautiful crucifixes. One can always distinguish a Pie crucifix from other crucifixes created by other artists, because, on a Pie crucifix, the head of Jesus is blissfully listed to one side... almost like a child sleeping, with a tremendous look of serenity on his face.

"Father, into your hands I commit my spirit."

"I brought them all back home."

"All back home."

Could you ever imagine that all of mankind might be saved by a single drop of blood?

Do you recall when, in the month of January, the Feast of the Circumcision was celebrated?

I wish we still celebrated the Feast of the Circumcision, because it marked the first drops of His precious blood being shed. And just one of those drops would have been enough to have redeemed a thousand worlds. So, why not let it end there?

The answer is, of course, mankind needed to learn to abandon itself to God... like Jesus did. We needed to learn how to give all... to learn how to give not a little, not a lot, but everything.

Everything.

I read a wonderful line not long ago. It went like this: *If I obey You because I want to go to heaven, then deny me heaven. If I serve You because I fear going to Hell, then send me to Hell. If I love You only to please me, then give me me. But if I obey You and serve You and love You because You are You, then... give me You.*

That is the mystery and some of us still do not get it.

The mystery is simply this: God is enough.

God is enough.

It is Good Friday because you and I have to come to the realization that someone died for us. He was not just anybody. He was the Son of God. And if you had been the only person in the world... still, He would have died for you.

Today, I leave you with two words that I would like you to carry away with you: "To" and "For."

And here is how I would like you to use those words:

God gave Himself "to" me and God gave Himself "for" me.

Help me to give myself "to" God, "for" the service of the Church.

On Good Friday Catholics are asked to venerate the Cross. We venerate the Cross with a kiss because the Man on the Cross kissed us and saved us. And then that God... the hidden God who was in the burning bush... the God who was hidden in that broken, bruised, and spat upon Jewish man... is now the God who lives in bread... and we will receive Him.

Soon enough it will also be time for us to give our God the only thing He really wants... just you.

What will you get in return?

God is enough.

Fr. Lavalley

Stations of the Cross

I
Jesus is condemned to death

We adore thee oh Christ and we praise you...

It had been an awful night... the night before. Yet, it started out so very beautifully. The night began with the Holy Eucharist; it began with supper. The night began with the feast of Passover.

Then... a morsel of bread that became the morsel of betrayal. Things grew worse from thereon.

There was the agony in the garden... and bitter, bitter loneliness.

There was desertion. There was the kiss from a friend... a kiss of betrayal; a kiss that blistered. And God alone knows what happened to Jesus while He was imprisoned.

We know about the crowning of thorns. We know about the scourging at the pillar. We know about the spit in the face of God. We know about the old rag thrown around His shoulders... the pretense of a king's cloak. And we know about the reed in His hand.

How far would drunken centurions go... and when would they stop?

There is something about our human nature that can be very, very good... or we can get carried away, can we not? We can get carried away with hate. We can get carried away with bitterness. We can get carried away with revenge.

Then... there was the next morning. Perhaps just being out of the jail was a release for Him... yet, He was displayed on a dais, whereupon, a crowd yelled and screamed and laughed at such a sight as was done to Him throughout the night.

It is amazing, is it not, the things we sometimes find amusing.

He stood in front of the crowd, because you and I needed Him to be there. He stood there trusting His Father and loving us all the while. When you trust God... when you love the people in your life... that is what you do. You stand there... even though you want to run.

Oh Jesus, by this first Station of the Cross help us to understand the meaning of a word that is used very loosely these days... when seldom used at all: "Duty."

Christ... as you stood there before the jeering throng... help us to stand.

Hail Mary, full of grace the Lord is with thee.

Blessed are you among all women,

And blessed is the fruit of thy womb, Jesus.

Holy Mary, mother of God,

Pray for us sinners,

Now, and at the hour of our death.

Amen.

Mary, mother of sorrow, pray for us.

II
Jesus takes up His Cross

We adore thee oh Christ and we praise you...

His was not the only cross. Crucifixion was a Roman sport. Crucifixion was a way of keeping people in line. When you have enough power, when you have a big enough fist, there is always a way to keep people in line. One of the ways the Romans kept their dissenters in line was through crucifixion.

Probably, the crosses were stored. One cross was really no different from another. His cross was different, however, not because it was made of different wood, but because of the hands that picked it up and embraced it.

Such a cross we venerate, because it was His Cross.

We venerate His Cross, because on that cross the world was redeemed and we were saved. He made it so that great sinners could become saints; little ones and big ones.

You and I will never be offered a whole cross all at once; we are not strong enough to handle such. We receive little splinters of our cross, here and there. Some splinters are bigger than others, but through the years those little splinters gradually form a whole cross were we to piece them all together. And if we carry our splinters the way He carried His Cross, we will be a better people for it. We will become holy and the world will become a better place.

Oh... we are not ready for the whole cross right now, but through our acceptance of our little splinters, if we carry them for love of Him, it will make a tremendous difference in our lives and in our world.

Saint Therese of Lisieux once said, "There is more accomplished through suffering than by a thousand servants."

Hail Mary, full of grace the Lord is with thee.
Blessed are you among all women,
And blessed is the fruit of thy womb, Jesus.
Holy Mary, mother of God,
Pray for us sinners,
Now, and at the hour of our death.
Amen.

Mary, mother of sorrow, pray for us.

III
Jesus falls the first time

We adore thee oh Christ and we praise you...

The Son of God fell to his knees on a dirty street. Perhaps He fell into a ditch. The streets were not clean in those days. The Son of God stumbled and fell amid the filth. Yet... that too was for us.

I wonder if anyone pushed Him.

Or tripped Him.

Sometimes what we perceive as humorous is anything but. My God... the things at which we can laugh.

In our lives, you and I are going to meet people in the ditch. We are going to meet people who have fallen. Such meetings present us with several options to act upon. One option, of course, is to pretend that we do not see the fallen ones. We can cross the street. What is their misery to do with us anyway?

But, there is a worse thing that we can do.

We can beat those who have fallen.

We are quite capable of doing such things, you know. We have done it to individuals. We have done it to races. We have done it to nations.

Sometimes we become judges.

I was recalling.. just now... a young gay man named Matthew Shepherd, who... like you and like me... was created in the image of God. Yet, several supposedly rational human beings, also created in the image of God, decided the world would be a better place without Matthew in it. They beat Matthew to death.

Yet, now I recall a little, old, withered, wrinkled-faced woman, who decided the people who were fallen in the death houses of Calcutta could be lifted up.

Ultimately, those are three choices between which we have to choose. We can ignore those who have fallen. We can beat those who have fallen. Or we can reach out to the fallen ones and lift them from whence they have fallen onto the dirty street.

Dear Lord... help us to understand the meaning of The Fall.

Hail Mary, full of grace the Lord is with thee.
Blessed are you among all women,
And blessed is the fruit of thy womb, Jesus.
Holy Mary, mother of God,
Pray for us sinners,
Now, and at the hour of our death.
Amen.

Mary, mother of sorrow, pray for us.

IV
Jesus meets His mother

We adore thee oh Christ and we praise you...

They are all difficult stations... but this particular station is a tough one.

This one is difficult.

Obviously, I have no way of knowing... but sometimes I think that as our Lord and Savior turned the corner and encountered our Lady, His mother, something within Him would have wanted to cry out, "Mama!"

Yet, at the same time... another something within Him would have wanted to plead to His Father, "Heavenly Father, I can do this, but please do not let her see me this way..."

Our Lady would have cried out, "Yashuwah!"

That is how Mary would have addressed her little Jesus in their native tongue.

"Yashuwah"... it is a child's name.

Our Lady could do nothing to stop this atrocity from continuing, so why was she there?

She was there, because she is always there.

Always.

I remember one occasion of being terribly embarrassed as a child. I was learning nursery rhymes in elementary school and I called out to the teacher proclaiming that I knew a nursery rhyme written about Jesus' mother.

It is funny what children will recall from childhood, is it not?

The teacher asked me to tell the class the name of the nursery rhyme.

I replied, "Mary had a little lamb."

Everyone in the room laughed; not unkindly... but enough so that I realized my mistake.

Years later... while I was in the seminary... by and through the course of my studies, I realized I had not erred after all. Mary really did have a little lamb. It was the Lamb of God. And everywhere the Lamb went... Mary was sure to go.

No one brings us closer to Jesus than does Mary. At this station we ask our Lady to bring us closer to Jesus and to help us stay by Him as she did.

Hail Mary, full of grace the Lord is with thee.
Blessed are you among all women,
And blessed is the fruit of thy womb, Jesus.
Holy Mary, mother of God,
Pray for us sinners,
Now, and at the hour of our death.
Amen.

Mary, mother of sorrow, pray for us.

V
Simon of Cyrene helps Jesus by carrying His Cross

We adore thee oh Christ and we praise you...

What a wonderful privilege it was to have been able to carry the Cross of Christ.

I wonder if Simon of Cyrene knew Jesus. The Gospel according to Saint Luke informs us that Simon was coming in from the fields. Perhaps he had been working and was just finished with his work. Was he in the wrong place at the wrong time... or was he in the right place at the right time?

Have you ever felt that you were in the wrong place at the wrong time?

Have you ever said aloud, but to no one in particular... why me?

Have you ever wished someone else would do that which was asked of you or that which is expected of you?

Take a good hard look at Simon of Cyrene. What if it had been you, who were carrying the Cross, and Simon said to you, "I am in the wrong place at the wrong time."

Could you not imagine yourself saying to him, "Hey buddy... take a good look over here just for a minute."

We all have our chance to carry the Cross. Such a chance is not going to present itself two thousand years ago... or two thousand years from now. Such a chance is going to present itself today. Such a chance is going to be in our town... in our city... in our place of work... on our street... in our school... down our lane; not on the 14th of Nicene, two thousand years ago, but right now. Someone needs you. Someone's cross is too heavy to bear. Whether you like that someone... or not... has absolutely nothing to do with any of it, because it is Christ. There are no mistakes in the Providence of God. There is no wrong place at the wrong time.

There are no mistakes in the Providence of God.

Shoulder the burden.

The burden is Christ.

Hail Mary, full of grace the Lord is with thee.
Blessed are you among all women,
And blessed is the fruit of thy womb, Jesus.
Holy Mary, mother of God,
Pray for us sinners,
Now, and at the hour of our death.
Amen.

Mary, mother of sorrow, pray for us.

VI
Veronica wipes the face of Jesus

We adore thee oh Christ and we praise you...

She has a lot to learn... this one. Veronica is a ditz. Take a look at her for heaven's sake. She ran out in front of a mob to wipe the face of a condemned prisoner. She interfered with a Roman crucifixion. It is a wonder she was not arrested herself. And, all of that aside, what earthly good could she possibly have thought she was going to accomplish by wiping the face of a man who was to going to continue bleeding and would be dead within hours anyway?

Did she really believe she was going to stop the blood from running down His face with her dirty, old veil?

What earthly purpose was there in what she had done?

None.

There was not one single earthly purpose in her gesture whatso-ever. There was a divine purpose in what she had done.

Her's was an act of love. Her's was an act of compassion. Her's was an act of kindness. Her action speaks to the little things in everyday life.

Veronica was magnificent. She was wonderful. She was the type of person who makes life worth living. She made little things count a great deal.

And legend has it that when Veronica took her veil home and un-folded it... she did not see just blood... she did not see just sweat... she did not see just dirt. She saw the Holy Face.

When you and I emulate Veronica... the Holy Face is impressed not on our veils or on our handkerchiefs, but on our souls. And we begin to emulate Jesus.

Hail Mary, full of grace the Lord is with thee.
Blessed are you among all women,
And blessed is the fruit of thy womb, Jesus.
Holy Mary, mother of God,
Pray for us sinners,
Now, and at the hour of our death.
Amen.

Mary, mother of sorrow, pray for us.

VII
Jesus falls the second time

We adore thee oh Christ and we praise you...

At the first fall we considered the people whom we meet... those who have fallen. Now, let us take a look at the second fall and consider someone else. This station is about me and it is about you.

Sometimes we are not the passer by. Sometimes we are the one in the ditch.

Sometimes we fall physically... sometimes we fall morally. Sometimes we are discouraged... sometimes we fall emotionally.

But we all fall.

Sometimes when we fall we are too embarrassed to look up. Sometimes the easiest thing for us to do is to lay in the ditch where we have fallen.

Sometimes...

And sometimes we just do not know how to raise ourselves from the fall... how to climb out of the ditch. That is why our Lord is with us.

When you are down, you are not alone. Reach out your hand. You will touch another hand. It is God's hand. It is Jesus' hand. Let Him help raise you up.

You say you cannot do it alone?

Of course you cannot... that is what Jesus is for.

Hail Mary, full of grace the Lord is with thee.
Blessed are you among all women,
And blessed is the fruit of thy womb, Jesus.
Holy Mary, mother of God,
Pray for us sinners,
Now, and at the hour of our death.
Amen.

Mary, mother of sorrow, pray for us.

VIII
Jesus consoles the women of Jerusalem

We adore thee oh Christ and we praise you...

Is that not ironic?

Jesus consoled the women of Jerusalem.

Who is taking care of who?

Considered the condition of Jesus at that moment... yet, He took time to console them.

Why?

Because that is what He does. It flows from who He is.

He consoles, because that is what He does.

What do we do?

We need to look at ourselves.   We need to ask hard questions of ourselves. You see... we form habits in life and those habits become a way of life.

There are habits in our lives that are evil; habits within which we often find ourselves trapped. Such habits are known as "habitual sin." And the only way habitual sin can be overcome is by replacing those habits with other habits known as "habitual virtue." This takes time. This takes practice. And it is much harder for us to replace habitual sin with habitual virtue, because habitual virtue is not as much fun as habitual sin.

Habitual sin may be more fun than habitual virtue... but habitual virtue is of much greater value.

The commonality of sinful pleasures is that the pleasure does not last. The initial pleasure may be extremely intense... but it does not last. The high is high... but not forever.

We need to look at our lives and we need to ask ourselves this question: Who am I?

Am I truly a follower of Christ?

Am I truly a Christian?

I recall a question posed by a very learned man of God; one who gave us a wonderful examination of conscience. He was speaking before a group of people and he said, "For a moment, I would like for you to pretend that you have been arrested by a state authority that is intent on stamping out Christianity. Pretend you are taken before a magistrate who is going to put you on trial for being a Christian. Imagine, if you can... will the magistrate possess enough evidence to condemn you?"

Will the magistrate be able prove the charge of being a Christian as it is made against you?

Jesus consoles, because that is what He does.

What do we do...?

Hail Mary, full of grace the Lord is with thee.
Blessed are you among all women,
And blessed is the fruit of thy womb, Jesus.

Holy Mary, mother of God,

Pray for us sinners,

Now, and at the hour of our death.

Amen.

Mary, mother of sorrow, pray for us.

IX
Jesus falls the third time

We adore thee oh Christ and we praise you...

During our reflection on the first station, we invoked a word that is not very popular these days: "Duty." At this station let us invoke another word that is not often used: "Perseverance."

Perseverance... it even has a nice sound to it. Perseverance is to persevere... to stay with... to go all the way... to stick with it...

We are always searching for clauses to relieve ourselves of our responsibilities. Sometimes we search for guarantees which Providence simply is not going to give us.

It is all about trusting God.

Jesus fell at the beginning of His journey to His crucifixion. He fell a second time during the middle of His journey to His crucifixion. He falls a third time at the end of His journey to His crucifixion.

The beginning... the middle... and the end. That is life, is it not?

Perseverance.

When I was a child, I possessed a simple book that told the story of a little engine that could. Have you read it?

Have you read the story of the little engine that thought it could climb to the top of a high hill.

If so, do you recall what the little engine repeated to itself during its climb up the mountain?

"I think I can... I think I can... I think I can... I think I can... I think I can... I think I can..."

Do you recall what the little engine repeated to itself during its descent from the mountain?

"I knew I could... I knew I could... I knew I could..."

Yes... I think we can!

Hail Mary, full of grace the Lord is with thee.
Blessed are you among all women,
And blessed is the fruit of thy womb, Jesus.
Holy Mary, mother of God,
Pray for us sinners,
Now, and at the hour of our death.
Amen.

Mary, mother of sorrow, pray for us.

X

Jesus is stripped of His garments

We adore thee oh Christ and we praise you...

In the humanity of Jesus, He was a Jew. The Jews are a very modest people. Among other things, they have a great respect for the human body.

Let us spend this moment in contemplation of this Roman nonsense... this blasphemy... to strip the Son of God, publicly; in front of His mother... in front of His followers... in front of the whole world.

We are so very polite in our paintings and in our statues of the crucifixion. We give Him loin cloths to wear.

We are so very polite, but that is not how Roman crucifixions were conducted.

Would it not have been wonderful to have covered Him?

Can we cover Him still?

I think we can.

I think we can cover Him in many different ways.

One of the ways of covering Him, perhaps, is through charity. There are still so many people in this world who suffer without sufficient food or clothing. That, my dear friends, is the stripped Christ.

There are so many people in this world who are homeless. There are so many people in this world who fail to possess something as simple as water... let alone clean water.

Clothe Christ.

Do you not find it amazing how little money we put into taking care of the naked Christ... and the hungry Christ... but the citizens of our beloved nation spend billions of dollars every year on a market that is scurrilously created for superficial personal pleasure: Pornography.

Pornography is a multi-billion dollar industry... and money flows into its market unabated.

And the people who are involved in that vile market... well... they are the Body of Christ as well. All manner of men, women, and children are drawn into that vile market. God alone knows what brought them to it... but they, too, are the Body of Christ.

My body and your body... we are the Body of Christ.

There are so many ways we can clothe the Body of Christ.

What are we going to do...?

Hail Mary, full of grace the Lord is with thee.
Blessed are you among all women,
And blessed is the fruit of thy womb, Jesus.
Holy Mary, mother of God,
Pray for us sinners,
Now, and at the hour of our death.
Amen.

Mary, mother of sorrow, pray for us.

XI
Jesus is nailed to the Cross

We adore thee oh Christ and we praise you...

Whenever we begin mass, the first gesture of our mass is not the sign of the Cross. The first gesture of our mass is the kissing of the Altar... and that is how our mass is ended, as well. By kissing the wood of the Altar, the wood of the Cross, we acknowledge the supreme sacrifice our Lord and Savior Jesus Christ made for the salvation of our souls.

Only in the death of Jesus is the priest and the victim the same. The victim is Christ. The priest who offers is Christ. Every time we come to mass we renew the sacrifice our Lord and Savior Jesus Christ made for the salvation of our souls.

On the very first night of my life in the seminary Father Augustin gave those of us new to the seminary an assignment. He told us that we could work on the assignment together. For our assignment, Father Augustin said, " I want you to do some research, and I want you to tell me how many priests there are in the United States."

Off we went with our books, and God alone knows what other reference material we poured over. When we returned to class the next day ready to turn in our papers with our answers so neatly written upon them, Father

Augustin said, "Good. Now, I would like you to continue your research tonight and tell me how many priests there are in the world."

So... off we went and the following day we brought in our findings to him. Much to our shock and dismay Father Augustin took all of our work and tossed it into the wastepaper basket. Hours and hours of research went into the garbage.

Father Augustin looked us over and said, "Now you begin your education. I am starting it now and we will continue it for eight years."

"There is only one priest in the whole wide world: Jesus Christ. When you stand at the Altar you are in Persona Christi... the person of Christ. You will have to teach yourselves and your people that we are all a part of that great mystery. Somehow you will have to teach yourselves and your people not to be afraid to lay on the Altar."

Nails did not hold our Lord and Savior to the Cross. It was love: His love for us.

Love held our Christ to the Cross.

The nails... they were a Roman indulgence.

I read a vignette once of a man who stood before Jesus and proclaimed himself to be a follower of Christ. Jesus looked at that man and said, "Let me see your hands and your feet."

The man turned his hands over and showed his palms to our Lord. The man took off his shoes and socks, and showed his feet to our Lord. After a moment, Jesus said to the man, "There are no wounds. Could you have traveled far, you who have no wounds... no scar?"

Lord... may we live the mass we celebrate... each and every day of our lives.

Hail Mary, full of grace the Lord is with thee.
Blessed are you among all women,
And blessed is the fruit of thy womb, Jesus.
Holy Mary, mother of God,
Pray for us sinners,
Now, and at the hour of our death.
Amen.

Mary, mother of sorrow, pray for us.

XII
Jesus dies on the Cross

We adore thee oh Christ and we praise you...

The Cross became something else. It became a pulpit. His last words became His last will and testimony.

A condemned man is always asked, "Do you have anything to say before you die?"

Jesus had something to say.

"Father, forgive them, for they know not what they do."

"Truly, I say to you, today you will be with me in Paradise."

"Eli, Eli, lema sabachthani?"

"My God, my God, why have you forsaken me?"

"Woman, behold, your son!"   *"Behold, your mother!"*

"I thirst."

He thirsts... for souls... for your love...

"Father, into your hands I commit my spirit."

"Consumato est."

"It is finished."

And, breathing a sigh, He gave up the ghost.

Lo'... there He hangs,
Ashen figure pinned against the wood.
Oh God... grant that I might love Him,
Even as I should.
I draw a little closer to share His love divine,
And hear Him softly murmur,
"Oh foolish child of mine."
"If now I should embrace you,
My hands would stain you red."
"And, if I should bend to kiss you,
My thorns would pierce your head."
Twas then I learned in meekness,
That love demands a price.
Twas then I knew that sorrow...
Was just the kiss of Christ.

Hail Mary, full of grace the Lord is with thee.
Blessed are you among all women,
And blessed is the fruit of thy womb, Jesus.
Holy Mary, mother of God,
Pray for us sinners,
Now, and at the hour of our death.
Amen.

Mary, mother of sorrow, pray for us.

XIII
Jesus is taken down from the Cross and is placed in the arms of His mother

We adore thee oh Christ and we praise you...

His life began in the arms of Mary... and His life ended in Mary's arms.

Do you know who was featured on the cover of the March 2006 issue of *Time* magazine?

Our Lady was.

In that particular edition, our Lady was the subject of the lead article. The article reported that the Catholic Church has honored our Lady for centuries, and now Protestant sects are beginning to honor her as well.

Her influence is spreading...

This station had to have been so very difficult for her.

One is gone and one has to stay.

The holy family was Jewish, and the Sabbath celebration was drawing near. To those of the Jewish faith this meant that the body of a corpse could not be touched... so the remains of the departed one had to be buried before the sun went down. Yet, there was no rushing Mary.

The artist, Michelangelo, saw this particular scene so very well... from his heart to his hand in the wonderful sculpture called the "Pieta." He sculpted a mother with her dead son in her arms... sitting there and holding her child for all the mothers of our world, who will hold dead children in their arms.

She held Jesus.

The story goes that Joseph of Arimathea asked, "We have to move quickly... what is she doing? What is taking so long?"

She was rocking Him... rocking Jesus. In some little way she was bringing Him back to Nazareth. She was holding Him close. Holding the lifeless, bruised body of her son. A son who was bone of her bone, flesh of her flesh. A son whom she had nurtured, and loved, and tucked beneath the covers at night.

Oh Mother of God... take us into your arms as well.

Without you there is no hope.

Hail Mary, full of grace the Lord is with thee.
Blessed are you among all women,
And blessed is the fruit of thy womb, Jesus.
Holy Mary, mother of God,
Pray for us sinners,
Now, and at the hour of our death.
Amen.

Mary, mother of sorrow, pray for us.

XIV
Jesus is buried

We adore thee oh Christ and we praise you...

The death of Jesus was not the end of anything. It was the beginning.

Jesus was taken from the Cross and was placed in a tomb; a tomb that did not even belong to Him. The tomb belonged to Joseph of Arimathea. It was a borrowed tomb. Joseph of Arimathea let Jesus use his tomb. That is alright for His purpose, however, because Jesus was not going to need it for very long. His occupancy of the tomb did not last. The only things that were left behind in the tomb were things of death: burial cloths, oils used to bathe the body, embalming fluids... death things.

And that is why we need to bury things that keep us from the Risen Christ.

Pontius Pilate and King Herod were well-pleased with what they had done... yet, we hear no more from them.

We hear no more of them.

Although it is natural for us to want to cry as we reflect upon the Stations of the Cross... God smiled upon us on that day... for God was only beginning His work. It is the mystery of our faith.

The Catholic Church... like Jesus Christ... dies and rises. Unlike Jesus Christ, however, the Church does so over and over and over again. It is a continual process. Throughout the history of the Church there have been those who have gleefully posted death notices for the Church... just as had been done for our Lord and Savior Jesus Christ.

"This is the end of it!" They are want to proclaim... so pleased with themselves for doing so.

The Romans thought they had killed it.

A multitude of persecutors throughout the ages thought they had killed it.

Communists thought they had killed it.

Fascists thought they had killed it.

Nazis thought they had killed it.

The death of the Catholic Church is announced time and time and time again.

All of the isms throughout the world continue to post their death notices. "The Church is dead!" They proclaim.

The spouse of the Church is the Risen Christ. We must never be discouraged when the Church falls upon hard times. There will always be dying times... but those are also beginnings, not ends.

The isms will never win out. Not ever. Jesus lives... the Church lives. And just when we are made to believe that the Church has died... something happens throughout the world and the dying Church rises once more. And while the prophets of doom never cease to clamor... you would think that after two-thousand years we would learn that the wake, they so merrily celebrate, is but a temporary one.

So... there they all were... gathered around the tomb... John and Peter, centurions and soldiers, Mary Magdalene and the other women. And they were all crying and weeping and wailing; except for one... There is absolutely nothing in Matthew, Mark, Luke, or John that mentions anything about our Lady being there.

Now... I know that our instinct would suggest she was gathered at the tomb with everyone else... but her presence is not even suggested. Of course the apostles would have mentioned it in their Gospels, had she been there. The point is she was not there. Why?

Why of all people closest to our Lord and Savior would not our Lady have been present at the tomb of her son?

Well, not only is our Lady the mother of the Son... she is the spouse of the Holy Spirit... she knows things. She is the seat of wisdom.

She is the Seat of Wisdom.

Where would she be?

She is a mother... and she is a Jewish mother at that. Someone has to cook dinner.

Guess who is coming for dinner...

Dear Mother Mary help us to always see your Risen Son and to never be discouraged by the Cross. Help us to know that there will always be a tomorrow morning.

Hail Mary, full of grace the Lord is with thee.
Blessed are you among all women,
And blessed is the fruit of thy womb, Jesus.
Holy Mary, mother of God,
Pray for us sinners,

Now, and at the hour of our death.
Amen.

Mary, mother of sorrow, pray for us.

Easter Vigil

A reading from the Book of Genesis:

In the beginning, when God created the heavens and the earth, the earth was a formless wasteland, and darkness covered the abyss, while a mighty wind swept over the waters.

Then God said, "Let there be light," and there was light. God saw how good the light was. God then separated the light from the darkness. God called the light "day," and the darkness he called "night." Thus evening came, and morning followed- the first day.

Then God said, "Let there be a dome in the middle of the waters, to separate one body of water from the other." And so it happened: God made the dome, and it separated the water above the dome from the water below it. God called the dome, "the sky." Evening came, and morning followed- the second day.

Then God said, "Let the water under the sky be gathered into a single basin, so that the dry land might appear." And so it happened: the water under the sky was gathered into its basin, and the dry land appeared. God called the dry land, "the earth," and the basin of the water he called "the sea." God saw how good it was.

Then God said, "Let the earth bring forth vegetation: every kind of plant that bears seed and every kind of fruit tree on earth that bears fruit with its seed in it." And so it happened: the earth brought forth every kind of plant that bears seed and every kind of fruit tree on earth that bears fruit with its seed in it. God saw how good it was. Evening came, and morning followed- the third day.

Then God said, "Let there be lights in the dome of the sky, to separate day from night. Let them mark the fixed times, the days and the years, and serve as luminaries in the dome of the sky, to shed light upon the earth." And so it happened: God made the two great lights, the greater one to govern the day, and the lesser one to govern the night; and he made the stars. God set them in dome of the sky, to shed light upon the earth, to govern the day and the night, and to separate the light from the darkness. God saw how good it was. Evening came and morning followed- the fourth day.

Then God said, "Let the water teem with an abundance of living creatures, and on earth let birds fly beneath the dome of the sky." And so it happened: God created the great sea monsters and all kinds of swimming creatures with which the water teems, and all kinds of winged birds. God saw how good it was, and God blessed them, saying, "Be fertile, multiply, and fill the water of the seas; and let the birds multiply on the earth." Evening came, and morning followed- the fifth day.

Then God said, "Let the earth bring forth all kinds of living creatures: cattle, creeping things, and wild animals of all kinds." And so it happened: God made all kinds of wild animals, all kinds of cattle, and all kinds of creeping things of the earth. God saw how good it was. Then God said, "Let us make man in our image, after our likeness. Let them have dominion over the fish of the sea, the birds of the air, and the cattle, and over all the wild animals and all the creatures that crawl on the ground." God created man in his image; in the image of God he created him; male and female he created them. God blessed them, saying, "Be fertile and multiply; fill the earth and subdue it. Have dominion over the fish of the sea, the birds of the air, and all the living things that move on the earth."

God also said, "See, I give you every seed-bearing plant all over the earth and every tree that has seed-bearing fruit on it to be your food; and to all the animals of the land, all the birds of the air, and all the living creatures that crawl upon the ground, I give you all the green plants for food." And so it happened. God looked at everything he had made, and found it very good. Evening came, and morning followed- the sixth day.

Thus the heavens and the earth and all their array were completed. Since on the seventh day God was finished with the work He had been doing, He rested on the seventh day from all the work He had undertaken.

A reading from the Book of Genesis:

God put Abraham to the test. He called to him, "Abraham!"

"Here I am," he replied.

Then God said, "Take your son Isaac, your only one, whom you love, and go to the land of Moriah. There you shall offer him up as a holocaust on a height that I will point out to you."

Early the next morning Abraham saddled his donkey, took with him his son Isaac and two of his servants as well, and with the wood that he had cut for the holocaust, set out for the place of which God had told him.

On the third day Abraham got sight of the place from afar. Then he said to his servants, "Both of you stay here with the donkey, while the boy and I go over yonder. We will worship and then come back to you."

Thereupon Abraham took the wood for the holocaust and laid it on his son Isaac's shoulders, while he himself carried the fire and the knife. As the two walked on together, Isaac spoke to his father Abraham, "Father!" Isaac said.

"*Yes, son,*" *he replied.*

"*Here are the fire and the wood, but where is the sheep for the holocaust?*" *Isaac asked.*

"*Son,*" *Abraham answered, "God himself will provide the sheep for the holocaust.*"

Then the two continued going forward.

When they came to the place of which God had told him, Abraham built an altar there and arranged the wood on it. Next he tied up his son Isaac, and put him on top of the wood on the altar. Then he reached out and took the knife to slaughter his son. But the Lord's messenger called to him from heaven, "Abraham, Abraham!"

"*Here I am,*" *he answered.*

"*Do not lay your hand on the boy,*" *said the messenger. "Do not do the least things to him. I know now how devoted you are to God, since you did not withhold from me your own beloved son.*"

As Abraham looked about, he spied a ram caught by its horns in the thicket. So he went and took the ram and offered it up as a holocaust in place of his son. Abraham named the site Yahweh-yireh; hence people now say, "On the mountain the Lord will see."

Again the Lord's messenger called to Abraham from heaven and said, "I swear by myself, declares the Lord, that because you acted as you did in not withholding from me your beloved son, I will bless you abundantly and make your descendants as countless as the stars of the sky and the sands of the seashore; your descendants shall take possession of the gates of their enemies, and in your descendants all the nations of the earth shall find blessing- all this because you obeyed my command."

A reading from the Book of Exodus:

The Lord said to Moses, "Why are you crying out to me? Tell the Israelites to go forward. And you, lift up your staff and, hand outstretched over the sea, split the sea in two, that the Israelites may pass through it on dry land. But I will make the Egyptians so obstinate that they will go in after them. Then I will receive glory through Pharaoh and all his army, his chariots and charioteers. The Egyptians shall know that I am the Lord, when I receive glory through Pharaoh and his chariots and charioteers."

The angel of God, who had been leading Israel's camp, now moved and went behind them. The column of cloud also, leaving the front, took up its place behind them, so that it came between the camp of the Egyptians and that of Israel. But the cloud now became dark, and thus night passed without the rival camps coming any closer together all night long. Then Moses stretched out his hand over the sea, and the Lord swept the sea with a strong east wind throughout the night and so turned it into dry land. When the water was thus divided, the Israelites marched into the midst of the sea on dry land, with the water like a wall to their right and to their left.

The Egyptians followed in pursuit; all Pharaoh's horses and chariots and charioteers went after them right into the midst of the sea. In the night watch just before dawn the Lord cast through the column of the fiery cloud upon the Egyptian force a glance that threw it into a panic; and he so clogged their chariot wheels that they could hardly drive. With that the Egyptians sounded the retreat before Israel, because the Lord was fighting for them against the Egyptians.

Then the Lord told Moses, "Stretch out your hand over the sea, that the water may flow back upon the Egyptians, upon their chariots and their charioteers."

So Moses stretched out his hand over the sea, and at dawn the sea flowed back to its normal depth. The Egyptians were fleeing head on toward the sea, when the Lord hurled them into its midst. As the water flowed back, it covered the chariots and charioteers of Pharaoh's whole army which had followed the Israelites into the sea. Not a single one of them escaped. But the Israelites had marched on dry land through the midst of the sea, with the water like a wall to their right and to their left. Thus the Lord saved Israel on that day from the power of the Egyptians. When Israel saw the Egyptians lying dead on the seashore and beheld the great power that the Lord had shown against the Egyptians, they feared the Lord and believed in him and his servant Moses.

Then Moses and the Israelites sang this song to the Lord: "I will sing to the Lord, for he is gloriously triumphant; horse and chariot he has cast into the sea."

A reading from the Book of the Prophet Isaiah:

"The One who has become your husband is your maker; his name is the Lord of Hosts; your redeemer is the Holy One of Israel, called God of all the earth. The Lord calls you back, like a wife forsaken and grieved in spirit, a wife married in youth and then cast off," says your God.

"For a brief moment I abandoned you, but with great tenderness I will take you back. In an outburst of wrath, for a moment I hid my face from you; but with enduring love I take pity on you," says the Lord, your redeemer.

"This is for me like the days of Noah, when I swore that the waters of Noah should never again deluge the earth; so I have sworn not to be angry with you, or to rebuke you. Though the mountains leave their place and the hills be shaken, my love for you shall never leave you nor my covenant of peace be shaken," says the Lord, who has mercy on you.

"O afflicted one, storm-battered and unconsoled, I lay your pavements in carnelians, and your foundations in sapphires; I will make your battlements of rubies, your gates of carbuncles, and all your walls of precious stones. All your children shall be taught by the Lord, and great

shall be the peace of your children. In justice shall you be established, far from the fear of oppression, where destruction cannot come near you."

A reading from the Letter of Saint Paul to the Romans:

Brothers and sisters: Are you unaware that we who were baptized into Christ Jesus were baptized into his death? We were indeed buried with him through baptism into death, so that just as Christ was raised from the dead by the glory of the Father, we too might live in the newness of life.

For if we have grown into union with him through death like his, we shall also be united with him in the resurrection. We know that our old self was crucified with him so that our sinful body might be done away with, that we might no longer be in slavery to sin. For a dead person has been absolved from sin. If, then, we have died with Christ, we believe that we shall also live with him. We know that Christ, raised from the dead, dies no more; death no longer has power over him. As to his death, he died to sin once and for all; as to his life, he lives for God. Consequently, you too must think of yourselves as being dead to sin and living for God in Christ Jesus.

A reading from the holy Gospel according to Matthew:

After the Sabbath, as the first day of the week was dawning, Mary Magdalene and the other Mary came to see the tomb. And behold, there was a great earthquake; for an angel of the Lord descended from heaven, approached, rolled back the stone, and sat upon it. His appearance was like lightning and his clothing was white as snow. The guards were shaken with fear of him and became like dead men. Then the angel said to the women in reply, "Do not be afraid! I know that you are seeking Jesus the crucified. He is not here, for he has been raised just as he said. Come and see the place where he lay. Then go quickly and tell his disciples, 'He has been raised from the dead, and he is going to Galilee; there you will see him.' Behold, I have told you."

Then they went away quickly from the tomb, fearful yet overjoyed, and ran to announce this to his disciples. And behold, Jesus met them on their way and greeted them. They approached, embraced his feet, and did him homage. Then Jesus said to them, "Do not be afraid. Go tell my brothers to go to Galilee, and there they will see me."

It is all about two words: Sanctifying Grace- God's life within us.

In today's Easter Vigil readings we read about the history of God and his people. And the reoccurring theme throughout is the fact that God entered into the life of His people. From the very beginning, in the Garden of Eden, to Abraham and his call from the order of Caldeas to form a people, to the deliverance of the Jewish people from bondage... God is with His people.

God works in ways by which we are never sure. God works in mysterious ways. And that is what we are celebrating today: the Paschal mystery- the dying and the rising of Jesus Christ.

On the back wall of Saint Francis Xavier church there is a painting of Jesus raising Lazarus from the dead. Although that was a wonderful event, it is not like the event we are celebrating on this Easter Vigil, because what we are celebrating here has absolutely no provision to it. It is new life. It is new creation. Jesus really and truly died on the Cross. His death was real. His burial was real. He died so that we might live. He died so that we might have life and have life more abundantly.

The very last words of the Risen Christ are these: *"Go into the world and make disciples of all nations. Baptize them in the name of the Father and of the Son and of the Holy Spirit. Teach them to carry out everything that I command you. And know that I am with you all days, even to the end of the age."*

It is about new life... a new creation.

When we receive baptism we receive the very life of the Risen Christ in our soul. We receive the very life of God. And what you and I are celebrating during this Easter Vigil is symbolized by the Paschal candle. It is symbolic in that from the Paschal candle we light all of the other candles within our church. All light comes from that one flame. Through the mystery of Baptism we can truly call God, our "Father", and Jesus, our "Brother."

During the Easter Vigil we celebrate the recommitment of our baptism. We renew our personal baptismal vows and promises. For some of you, your baptism was not that long ago. For others, it was many, many years ago. We are asked to remember the Communion of Saints. We are asked to remember those people who went before us, our loved ones. And though it is customary for us to describe their passing by saying they died, I say to you, "No they did not."

They have a stronger and better life now than we have because they have the fullness of grace. And grace becomes glory. In the most simplest ways imaginable the Communion of Saints means one thing:

We are all together.

Fr. Lavalley

Easter Sunday,
The Resurrection of the Lord

A reading from the Acts of the Apostles.

Peter proceeded to speak and said, "You know what has happened all over Judea, beginning in Galilee after the baptism that John preached, how God anointed Jesus of Nazareth with the Holy Spirit and power. He went about doing good and healing all those oppressed by the devil, for God was with him. We are all witnesses of all that he did both in the country of the Jews and in Jerusalem. They put him to death by hanging him on a tree. This man God raised on the third day and granted that he be visible, not to all the people, but to us, the witnesses chosen by God in advance, who ate and drank with him after he rose from the dead. He commissioned us to preach to the people and testify that he is the one appointed by God as judge of the living and the dead. To him all the prophets bear witness, that everyone who believes in him will receive forgiveness of sins through his name."

A reading from the Letter of Saint Paul to the Colossians.

Brothers and sister: If then you were raised with Christ, seek what is above, where Christ is seated at the right hand of God. Think of what is above, not of what is on earth. For you have died, and your life is hidden with Christ in God. When Christ your life appears, then you too will appear with him in glory.

A reading from the holy Gospel according to John.

On the first day of the week, Mary of Magdala came to the tomb early in the morning, while it was still dark, and saw the stone removed from the tomb. So she ran and went to Simon Peter and to the other disciple whom Jesus loved, and told them, "They have taken the Lord from the tomb, and we don't know where they put him." So Peter and the other disciple went out and came to the tomb. They both ran, but the other disciple ran faster than Peter and arrived at the tomb first; he bent down and saw the burial cloths there, but did not go in. When Simon Peter arrived after him, he went into the tomb and saw the burial cloths there, and the cloth that had covered his head, not with the burial cloths but rolled up in a separate place. Then the other disciple also went in, the one who had arrived at the tomb first, and he saw and believed. For they did not yet understand the Scripture that he had to rise from the dead.

Let us begin our Easter celebration by talking about the wonderful feast we are meant to celebrate. What is the reality of our Easter celebration?

One of the first things we are taught as Christians is that Jesus died and Jesus rose from the dead into new life. Yet, in today's Gospel reading we learn that the disciples did not grasp what that fundamental basis of Christianity meant. In fact, whenever Jesus spoke to His disciples of His death and His resurrection, they always had questions. Thereto, it is not in our experience for someone to die and to rise to new life.

You and I have been guided in our belief of the Dying and Risen Christ from the beginning of our Christian life. We accept and believe in it, but we do not fully understand it. That is what is so important about this Easter season. Step by step, we are guided to understand a little bit more about the Risen Christ.

At the beginning of today's mass my prayer for you was the fullness of a risen life. Through Catechism, we are taught that at Baptism we die with Christ, and we are risen with Him to new life. Through our baptism we become a new being... a new creation. In a very real sense, a baby that is brought to the Church to be baptized is not the same baby that will be taken home. A new life has been given to him or her.

Prior to Baptism, a baby possessed human life that was shared with him or her by the mother and father. Through the Sacrament of Baptism, God gives that baby a share of divine life.

What is divine life?

Is life the same as it always was or is there something new about the life that is given to us through Baptism?

At our baptism, you and I shared in the risen life of Jesus... not the dead life... the risen life. We live with a new life, one that has been given to us. It is not something for which we have to work. It is simply something that we accept and live. And that is what we do when we consciously learn to say this is the choice I make to follow Jesus.

At the conclusion of today's homily I will ask all of us to renew the commitment we made at our baptism, a commitment that was made for us by either our parents, grandparents, or godparents. And when we renew our baptismal commitment I would like you to listen to the spoken words carefully... to be mindful of what we are doing... and to make it very real for you today.

We share in the risen life of Christ.

Not someday down the road.

Now!

When we die, we are born again into eternity. Eternity is a new aspect of living the risen life which you and I already possess within us.

In the first chapter of his letter to the Ephesians, Saint Paul wrote about the spiritual blessings of Christ. He wrote that the very power that raised Jesus from the dead was at work in those who believe. And that is why, at the beginning of today's Easter celebration, we proclaimed through song, "This is the day that the Lord has made. Let us rejoice and be glad."

The reality of our Easter celebration is essentially this: the power it took to raise Jesus... who really died... who really was buried... who really was raised up to new life on the third day... really is at work in you and in me, today.

To that end, I am going to attempt to provide you with an example. And I stress that my example is merely an example; something that is like something else.

To those of you old enough to remember such doings, do you recall the dropping of the atomic bombs upon Hiroshima and Nagasaki?

I was ten years old when that horrific event occurred, but I still vividly recall the photographs taken in the aftermath; photographs published in the local newspaper.

One of the photographs I recall seeing was taken of a leaking water pipe. The image of the pipe was not a photograph of the pipe itself, rather it was an image of the pipe burned into the wall by the explosion. The tremendous power of the atomic blast burned the image of the pipe, its shadow if you will, onto the surface of one of the walls within which the pipe was located.

Another photograph that comes to mind was taken of a human hand; a hand raised with its fingers outstretched. Again, that photograph was not of an actual hand, but of an image burned onto a wall of a room, presumably, within which that human being had been at the time of the blast. The tremendous power of the atomic blast burned a shadow of a human being's hand onto a wall.

Much discussion has come to pass regarding the authenticity of the Holy Shroud of Turin. The discussions often center over whether or not the Holy Shroud of Turin is the actual burial cloth of Jesus Christ. On the one hand, most theologians and persons of faith have come to believe the Holy Shroud of Turin is the actual burial cloth of Jesus. On the other hand, however, many scholars and scientists dispute the authenticity of the Shroud.

Scientists at the Los Alamos laboratory in New Mexico, where the first atomic bomb was developed, have advanced a theory as to how the image, we believe to be that of Jesus Christ, came to be imprinted upon the Holy Shroud of Turin. Their hypothesis is that when the power of God reentered the dead body of Jesus and rose it to new life, the power of that transformation was so great that it burned the image of Jesus onto the burial cloth. Something, perhaps, like the power that burned shadows of objects and human beings onto walls of buildings at the site of the atomic bomb detonations in Hiroshima and Nagasaki. In any event, this gives us an idea of what we are discussing today.

What happened at our baptism?

When you and I were baptized, the power of God... the life of God... entered into you and me, and we were born anew. As it was, the image of Jesus Christ was burned into our souls by the power of God. When God looks upon you and upon me, He witnesses our uniqueness, our beauty, our glory, our vulgarity, and our ignobility. Yet, when God looks upon you and upon me He also sees the face of His Son, Jesus.

That is what is meant by new life. That is the new life you and I are called to live.

Easter Sunday is a celebration of our new life.

So... not only should we rejoice and be glad on this day of new life, we must also allow the gravity of this day to sink into our psyche because once you realize who you are and I realize who I am we can never be the same again. That is the reality of the Resurrection. The Resurrection is not a pious tale. The Resurrection is not a story conceived to make us feel good about ourselves. The Easter celebration is a celebration of the Resurrection, but it is also a celebration of who we are and what we possess within ourselves.

In that spirit then, I ask each and everyone of you to go forth from this Easter celebration remembering who you are, and knowing that the very power that raised Jesus from the dead is at work in each of us who believe.

Let us end our Easter celebration this day by renewing our baptismal commitment to God, our baptismal commitment to our Lord and Savior Jesus Christ, and our baptismal commitment to the Church.

Through the paschal mystery we have been buried with Christ in Baptism, so that we may rise with Him to newness of life. Now that we have completed our Lenten observance, let us renew the promises we made in Baptism, when we rejected Satan and his works and promised to serve God faithfully in His holy Catholic Church.

Do you reject sin so as to live in the freedom of God's children?

Do you reject the glamor of evil and refuse to be mastered by sin?

Do you reject Satan, father of sin and prince of darkness?

Do you reject Satan?

And all his works?

And all his empty promises?

Do you believe in God, the Father Almighty, Creator of heaven and earth?

Do you believe in Jesus Christ, His only Son, our Lord, who was born of the Virgin Mary, was crucified, died, and was buried, rose from the dead, and is seated at the right hand of the Father?

Do you believe in the Holy Spirit, the holy Catholic Church, the Communion of Saints, the forgiveness of sins, the resurrection of the body, and the life everlasting?

God, the all-powerful Father of our Lord Jesus Christ, has given us a new birth by water and the Holy Spirit and forgiven all our sins. May He also keep us faithful to our Lord Jesus Christ for ever and ever. Amen.

Fr. Ragis

And the life of the world to come. Amen.

Second Sunday of Easter
Divine Mercy Sunday

A reading from the Acts of the Apostles:

They devoted themselves to the teaching of the apostles and to the communal life, to the breaking of bread and to the prayers. Awe came upon everyone, and many wonders and signs were done through the apostles. All who believed were together and had all things in common; they would sell their property and possessions and divide them among all according to each one's need. Every day they devoted themselves to meeting together in the temple area and to breaking bread in their homes. They ate their meals with exultation and sincerity of heart, praising God and enjoying favor with all the people. And every day the Lord added to their number those who were being saved.

A reading from the first Letter of Saint Peter:

Blessed be the God and Father of our Lord Jesus Christ, who in his great mercy gave us a new birth to a living hope through the resurrection of Jesus Christ from the dead, to an inheritance that is imperishable, undefiled, and unfading, kept in heaven for you who by the power of God are safeguarded through faith, to a salvation that is ready to be revealed in the final time. In this you rejoice, although now for a little while you may have to suffer through various trials, so that the genuineness of your faith, more precious than gold that is perishable even though tested by fire, may prove to be for praise, glory, and honor at the revelation of Jesus Christ. Although you have not seen him you love him; even though you do not see him now yet believe in him, you rejoice with an indescribable and glorious joy, as you attain the goal of your faith, the salvation of your souls.

A reading from the holy Gospel according to John:

On the evening of that first day of the week, when the doors were locked, where the disciples were, for fear of the Jews, Jesus came and stood in their midst and said to them, "Peace be with you." When he had said this he showed them his hands and his side. The disciples rejoiced when they saw the Lord. Jesus said to them again, "Peace be with you. As the Father has sent me, so I send you." And when he had said this, he breathed on them and said to them, "Receive the Holy Spirit. Whose sins you forgive are forgiven them, and whose sins you retain are retained."

Thomas, called Didymus, one of the Twelve, was not with them when Jesus came. So the other disciples said to him, "We have seen the Lord." But he said to them, "Unless I see the mark of the nails in his hands and put my finger into the nailmarks and put my hand into his side, I will not believe." Now a week later his disciples were again inside and Thomas was with them. Jesus came, although the doors were locked, and stood in their midst and said, "Peace be with you." Then he said to Thomas, "Put your finger here and see my hands, and bring your hand and put it in my side, and do not be unbelieving, but believe." Thomas answered and said to him, "My Lord and my God!" Jesus said to him, "Have you come to believe because you have seen me? Blessed are those who have not seen and have believed."

Now, Jesus did many other signs in the presence of his disciples that are not written in this book. But these are written that you may come to believe that Jesus is the Christ, the Son of God, and that through this belief you may have life in his name.

On this day, the second Sunday of Easter, we continue to celebrate the Resurrection of our Lord and Savior Jesus Christ, but this particular day, April 03, 2005, is also significant in that we are mourning the passing of the holy father, John Paul II. As I reflected over his passing, I thought, "There could not be a more appropriate line for this day than that found in the second reading of today's Scripture."

Although you have not seen him, you love him...

Most of us have seen John Paul II from a distance... from afar. The majority of us have never touched the man whom we have seen, but we loved him nonetheless. We loved him because of who he was.

Yesterday, before I came to the church to participate in the Sacrament of Reconciliation, I asked to be notified in the event the holy father died while I was at Saint Francis Xavier. And then, between penitence, the door opened ever so slightly, a head appeared, and a voice simply said, "The holy father just died."

At that moment I excused myself and went to the back of the church, whereupon, I tolled the bells for the passing of the pontiff. I returned to the front of the church where there were about a dozen people gathered waiting on me. Together we prayed for the departed soul of our holy father. I reentered the confessional and sat down... and the news of the pontiff's passing struck me in a way that such passings had never done before.

In dealing with the news of John Paul II's death, it occurred to me that while we knew his death was inevitable, as are the deaths of all of our loved ones, when you hear the actual words of it... that a loved one has died... such words appear as though one has not prepared for them at all.

I have always felt that way. Sitting there... in the confessional... in the dark... I recalled the death of Pius XII, John XXIII, Paul VI, and John Paul I, and I realized just how much like little children we really are. I felt the loss very deeply; a loss over losing my father... my father in Christ... the holy father. A natural sense of insecurity descended upon me.

And while I was sitting there, in the dark, dealing with all of those emotions, I heard a voice. The voice did not come from heaven... as you might suppose was my initial thought... no, the voice appeared at my side, whispering these words, "Bless me father for I have sinned."

My heart was overwhelmed with joy.

It still goes on.

Even when a pope dies.

It does not stop.

This marvelous thing called the Sacramental Life of the Church... nothing stops it.

Before this day, I was thinking about the Gospel readings for our Second Sunday of Easter celebration, and I thought, "Over two thousand years ago the Lord Jesus breathed on a band of sinful men and absolved them of their sinfulness."

How do you breathe on someone?

You hold them tight and your breath goes against their face.

I believe that is exactly what He did. He took everyone of them, one by one, and He breathed upon them. There was intimacy there... intimacy that breathes and allows fingers to go into wounds, and hands, and feet, and side.

We are called to intimacy with Christ.

Over two-thousand years ago Jesus Christ absolved people from sin, and He commanded His disciples to do the same, saying, *"Bring them home! Bring them to me! Bring my mercy!"*

What a wonderful and magnificent thing it is that this light of Christ, called the Church, does not stop. It cannot stop, because it is of God.

We mourn the passing of John Paul II, and in that mourning I switched on the television and heard many people say many beautiful things about the man. People from other faiths, other cultures, and other climates were saying things like, "What a wonderful humanitarian he was..."

Indeed, he was.

"And what a fighter for justice he was..."

Yes, he was.

"And what a charismatic man he was..."

Yes, he was that too.

"And what a strong advocate for life he was..."

Yes, very much so.

"And what a wonderful man he was for building bridges and tearing down walls, not only among the Communist states, but among churches..."

Yes, he was.

"And how beloved he was and praised by the Jewish rabbi who gave him a blessing, whom the holy father thanked for it..."

Yes, he was.

He was all that was said of him... and so much more.

He was the Vicar of Christ on earth. He was the Holy Father.

That is who he was...

It is always such a mystery when the election of a pope takes place. I recall being in Loretta, Pennsylvania, in the seminary, when the election of John Paul II was announced. It was noontime and I was waiting on table. Meals were eaten in silence, except that someone would read to us while we ate.

I recall Brother Amadeus. He was the cook. To my eyes he appeared as though he ate much more than he ever prepared. Brother Amadeus was a big man. Brother Amadeus entered the dining room on that day and yelled, "Shut up!"

Everyone looked up from their meals, and he said, "I think we've had an election."

Then, he grabbed me by the shoulder and said, "Go out and tell Father Roland."

Silence in the seminary was not to be disturbed or interrupted unless something of extreme importance occurred or was occurring. It could be argued that the election of a pope was extremely important.

I found Father Roland and said to him, "Excuse me father... but there has been an election."

Father Roland, who had just returned from Rome, looked up at me and asked, "Cardinal Montini...?"

I replied, "No, father... it is not Cardinal Montini."

"Well," he demanded. "Who is it?"

I replied, "It is Cardinal Roncalli."

Father Roland's face dropped. He said, "Roncalli from Venice..."

"Yes, father," I said.

"Oh my heaven," Father Roland replied. "He is an old man. He is decrepit. He will not do anything."

Cardinal Roncalli became Pope John XXIII... and he did many wonderful things. He was the man for the time.

The next election... Father Roland got it right. Cardinal Montini became Pope Paul VI.

I am going to share a story with you. It is a story about a man whose name is Daniel. I assure you that he is a real person, however, I will not divulge his last name.

When John Paul II traveled to the United States, for the first time, he went to New York City. At that time, Daniel was a young man in his early twenties. He was a baptized Catholic, who became very angry at many people and many things. Specifically, Daniel was angry with institutions and anything that reeked of authority. I suspect he will always have to deal with that anger on one level or another, but at that particular point in his life Daniel absolutely hated the Catholic Church. By proxy, he hated the holy father.

When Daniel learned of the Pope's visit to New York City, he was determined to awaken very early that morning so he could get a place on the curb in front Saint Patrick's Cathedral, on Fifth Avenue. Daniel was not intent on doing physical harm to the holy father, but what he wanted to do was to raise his hand and shout blasphemies at John Paul II... to curse John Paul II... and to do other such manner of vile things in the holy father's presence.

As the Pope's entourage traveled down Fifth Avenue and passed by Saint Patrick's Cathedral, Daniel raised his hand... just as he had planned. At that moment, the holy father turned his head and his gaze fell upon Daniel. Daniel's eyes were locked into the eyes of the holy father. Daniel fell to pieces. He ran into the crowd and sought out the nearest priest he could find. That priest brought Daniel into the doorway of a nearby store.... and right there... on Fifth Avenue... the priest heard Daniel's confession.

When those events took place I was the Vocation Director for the Diocese of Burlington.

Six months later Daniel was in my office telling me that story... and telling me that he wanted to become a priest. I asked, "What have you been doing for the past six months?"

Daniel replied, "I went down to a little bit of a hermitage where there was a priest on sabbatical, who had been living in solitude for a year. He has been helping me. And I have been traveling through New England..."

I said, "Tell me a little bit about your interaction with that priest."

And, he proceeded to do so.

At one point in our conversation, Daniel repeated something that the priest at the hermitage had told him. Immediately, I seized upon what Daniel had related and I asked him to repeat himself.

He did.

"You were with Father Augustin!" I exclaimed.

Daniel replied, "Yes I was. Do you know him?"

"Yes, Daniel," I said. "Yes, I know him."

Father Augustin is my spiritual advisor.

All of these things happen through divine providence.

Daniel never became a diocesan priest. He became a monk. And it all came to pass... because he looked into the eyes of the Polish Pope.

We mourn the loss of John Paul II.

All over the Catholic world many masses were held in observance of the holy father's passing. And while it is right to pray... and very good to pray... how many of our prayers do you think John Paul II needed?

If John Paul II has not made it to heaven... personally... I am more than a little concerned at my own prospects.

Soon after the passing of John Paul II, there was another man, who, among other such men, packed his bags for a trip to Rome. He packed his bags for a short trip, but he ended up embarking on a journey that will last much longer than he had anticipated. He left his home and he told his friends and family that he would see them in just a few short weeks... but he would not. He was destined to become the next Pope, and he would not return home even to collect his personal belongings.

And, on that first night in Rome when he occupied the Papal apartment... can you imagine how frightened that man was?

The only view he has is that of Saint Peter's Square.

We know he has been given the Crosier. What we do not fully realize is that he has been given the Cross.

He will be the right man for the job, you know... because the shoes he has to fill are not the shoes of John Paul II. To quote Morris West, "They are the shoes of the fisherman."

They are the shoes of Peter.

He will become our holy father, and all will be as it was before.

Why does the Sacramental Life of the Church go on unabated?

In the words of John Paul II... **The heart and the center and the life of the Catholic Church is the Holy Eucharist.**

Fr. Lavalley

We believe in one God, the Father, the Almighty, maker of heaven and earth, of all that is seen and unseen...

Third Sunday of Easter

A reading from the Acts of the Apostles:

Then Peter stood up with the Eleven, raised his voice, and proclaimed, "You who are Jews, indeed all of you staying in Jerusalem. Let this be known to you, and listen to my words. You who are Israelites, hear these words. Jesus the Nazorean was a man commended to you by God with mighty deeds, wonders, and signs, which God worked through him in your midst, as you yourselves know. This man delivered up by the set plan and foreknowledge of God, you killed, using lawless men to crucify him. But God raised him up, releasing him from the throes of death, because it was impossible for him to be held by it. For David says of him: 'I saw the Lord ever before me, with him at my right hand I shall not be disturbed. Therefore my heart has been glad and my tongue exulted; my flesh, too, will dwell in hope, because you will not abandon my soul to the netherworld, nor will you suffer your holy one to see corruption. You have made known to me the paths of life; you will fill me with joy in your presence.'"

"My brothers, one can confidently say to you about the patriarch David that he died and was buried, and his tomb is in our midst to this day. But since he was a prophet and knew that God had sworn an oath to him that he would set one of his descendants upon his throne, he foresaw and spoke of the resurrection of the Christ, that neither was he abandoned

to the netherworld nor did his flesh see the corruption. God raised this Jesus; of this we are all witnesses. Exalted at the right hand of God, he received the promise of the Holy Spirit from the Father and poured him forth, as you see and hear."

A reading from the first Letter of Saint Paul:

Beloved: If you invoke as Father him who judges impartially according to each one's works, conduct yourselves with reverence during the time of your sojourning, realizing that you were ransomed from your futile conduct, handed on by your ancestors, not with perishable things like silver or gold but with the precious blood of Christ as of a spotless unblemished lamb. He was known before the foundation of the world but revealed in the final time for you, who through him believe in God who raised him from the dead and gave him glory, so that your faith and hope are in God.

A reading from the holy Gospel according to Luke:

That very day, the first day of the week, two of Jesus' disciples were going to a village seven miles from Jerusalem called Emmaus, and they were conversing about all the things that had occurred. And it happened that while they were conversing and debating, Jesus himself drew near and walked with them, but their eyes were prevented from recognizing him. He asked them, "What are you discussing as you walk along?"

They stopped, looking downcast. One of them, named Cleopas, said to him in reply, "Are you the only visitor to Jerusalem who does not know of the things that have taken place there in these days?"

And he replied to them, "What sort of things?"

They said to him, "The things that happened to Jesus the Nazarene, who was a prophet mighty in deed and word before God and all the people, how our chief priests and rulers both handed him over to a sentence of death and crucified him. But we were hoping that he would be the one to redeem Israel; and besides all this, it is now the third day since this took place. Some women from our group, however, have astounded us: they were at the tomb early in the morning and did not find his body; they came back and reported that they had indeed seen a vision of angels who announced that he was alive. Then some of us went to the tomb and found things just as the women had described, but him they did not see."

And he said to them, "Oh, how foolish you are! How slow of heart to believe all that the prophets spoke! Was it not necessary that the Christ should suffer these things and enter into his glory?"

Then beginning with Moses and all the prophets, he interpreted to them what referred to him in all the Scriptures. As they approached the village to which they were going, he gave the impression that he was going on farther. But they urged him, "Stay with us, for it is nearly evening and the day is almost over."

So he went in to stay with them. And it happened that, while he was with them at table, he took bread, said blessing, broke it, and gave it to them. With that their eyes were opened and they recognized him, but he vanished from their sight. Then they said to each other, "Were our hearts not burning within us while he spoke to us on the way and opened the Scripture to us?"

So they set out at once and returned to Jerusalem where they found gathered together the eleven and those with them who were saying, "The Lord truly has been raised and has appeared to Simon!"

Then the two recounted what had taken place on the way and how he was made known to them in the breaking of bread.

What a magnificent change took place in Peter!

Recall, if you will, that in the Acts of the Apostles we read about an event that took place after the Resurrection and after Pentecost. And, what we learned about that event is that a complete change occurred in Peter, brought about by the power of the Holy Spirit. Peter was no longer a coward. Peter was no longer tepid. He was no longer timid; he was no longer frightened.

Peter was a disciple, he became an Apostle.

Peter discovered himself. He finally realized what he had been appointed to do in the Church. He was Peter... *"...you are Peter, and on this rock I will build my church and the gates of hell shall not prevail against it."*

Peter finally knew who he was, and he went forth with that knowledge with all kinds of courage. Why?

Because he had received the Holy Spirit.

What did Peter say?

In so many words, Peter said, "You were given a wonderful gift by the Father, and the gift you were given by the Father is called Jesus. And He came to save us. He came to redeem us. He came to love us."

Then, in the middle of his recitation, Peter threw a curve at his audience by saying, without blemish or fear, "Oh... and by the way... you killed him."

"You had cruel and wicked men do it... but you did it nonetheless."

How is that for cold water thrown in one's face?

Peter was not finished, though, and he went on from there to say, "It does not matter anyway because the Father had a plan, and in the Father's plan a child was raised up, brought to glory, and now sits at the right hand of the Father. He sits there for you."

What was Peter doing?

Peter was calling mankind to an awareness of our sinfulness and our need for the Savior. And that is not a depressing thing, because it is only through the awareness of sinfulness that we are going to find Grace, and realize how truly loved we are by God. If we do not think we need a Savior we will never find Grace.

If we are very patient... Grace will find us.

I am paraphrasing, of course, but in today's reading of the Gospel, Saint Peter said to the Israelites, "Oh, by the way, that God, who was your Creator, you can call Him "Father" if you want to... provided you walk in righteousness. And do not be discouraged about what I have told you... about you having killed Him... because it is by His love that you have been cleansed and made whole. You can receive the same Holy Spirit that was given to me and to the other Apostles."

That is why we are the Church... you and I... because we have received the Holy Spirit.

Let us take a look at the Gospel according to Saint Luke: the story of the two men. It is a story that teaches us who we are, collectively as the Church. In that Gospel reading we will discover a power we possess, but a power of which we may not be aware. It is a power that came to us in Baptism.

There were two disciples of Jesus... and the Gospel describes them as being downcast. They were downcast because they believed they had lost Jesus.

There is no tragedy in life worse than losing Jesus.

There is no greater joy than that in finding Him.

The disciples were downcast and they were on a road heading out of town. They were leaving Jerusalem. Yes... they had heard some women, who were known to the disciples, mention something about going to the tomb of Joseph of Arimathea, and discovering that the body of

Jesus was gone, but it is obvious from their reaction that they were not buying that old line. They might have been hoping for the Resurrection of Jesus to be true, but they were not buying it. They were leaving town.

While they were walking away from Jerusalem, they were conversing. They were talking with one another in an attempt at reconciling their experiences with this "Jesus" phenomena in a manner that made sense to them. They were blabbing with one another... going on and on and on and on... when all of a sudden a stranger appeared. The stranger joined them. He fell in step with them as they were walking along.

You see... that is how our Lord always begins. He gets in step with us- to get us in step with Him.

The disciples had no idea who that stranger was.

Have you ever been in shoes similar to those of the disciples?

Have you ever been downcast?

Have your eyes ever been downcast?

Has your heart ever been downcast?

Has your soul ever been downcast?

Have you ever thought you lost Jesus?

Have you ever wondered where God was?

Have you ever wondered why you could not find Him?

Perhaps one of the reasons we have a hard time finding God or hearing God is because we are doing precisely what those two disciples are doing.

We chatter too much.

We really do, you know.

We really chatter a lot.

We are people of noise.

Have you ever noticed that?

We absolutely love sound and are terrified of silence... real silence.

For some reason silence frightens us.

"Not true," say you.   Well, bear with me here for a moment.

When you get into your car, after you start the engine, what is the next thing you do?

What is turned on?

The radio, that's what. You turn on the radio or the compact disc player or the cassette tape player. Whatever has been installed in there... factory installed or custom built.

We need noise. We need to have our collections with us: our compact disc collections, or our cassette tape collections.

God forbid that we should be alone with our thoughts during our travels from point A to point B!

What do we do when we enter our homes?

We turn on our television sets. We do not want to be too far from our telephones, either.

God forbid we should be too far from our telephones!

These days we even carry our telephones around with us in our shirt or trouser pockets.

We absolutely worship noise... even good noise. Music is good noise.

But there is a place in our lives for absolute silence. We need real silence.

We need to be quiet.

One of these days you must take it upon yourselves to teach some-one something about prayer. Perhaps you need to teach yourself about prayer. Begin by asking your understudy to set aside fifteen minutes each day for quiet, peaceful meditation; just fifteen minutes. No music. No noise. No distractions. Nothing. Absolute quiet. Be alone. Ask your understudy to simply be alone with his or her thoughts and with those of our God.

Do not be surprised, when you ask if he or she was able to be com-pletely silent for fifteen minutes, if the answer is "No."

"Did you do it for fifteen minutes?"

"No."

"How long did you do it for?"

"Maybe five minutes."

(More likely than not, maybe two and a half minutes.)

"What made you stop?"

"I got bored."

In whose company were you?

Did that person with whom you were alone in silence bore you?

What does that say about you?

What does that say about us?

Does it say, "It is not possible for me to be alone with my thoughts and with my feelings?"

How very sad!

Let us go to the mystery of our faith.

There have been many studies over the years that have shown we have not fully developed our brain and have failed to tap into its fullest potential. I recall speaking with a priest who had done much work with Franciscan missions in India, and he became easily riled when people talked about Hindu rope tricks or walking on coals. He would reply, rather tersely, "There is no trick about it. It is not a trick. It is the mind."

We have all heard stories, or read stories, about a desperate mother who, upon seeing her child hopelessly trapped beneath a car, or a similarly impossibly heavy object, rushed over to the car, lifted it, and pulled her child to safety. From where does such strength come?

It is not a trick. It comes from the mind.

What I am going to suggest to you, today, is that there is a part of the soul we have not fully developed either.

All who believe are called to contemplative prayer.

All who believe...

Scary, is it not?

Alright... so let us erase the words "contemplative prayer" and consider our obligation in this manner: God desires of His children an intimate relationship; a mutual sharing of love.

Does that work better for you?

Too often we are very good at saying our prayers... of doing our novenas... of reciting our rosaries... of getting it all in. And not one of those things is bad. They are all very good things, but that is not all there is to us. The first quality of a spiritual life is silence... of being alone... of absolute silence.

We need to be on the road to Emmaus... but we need to walk in silence.

Can you look back on your life, right this minute, to those times when you thought you were alone, because you were either too busy with too many things or too overwhelmed with too much sorrow and too much downcastedness. Now, with the clarity of age and experience, can you see for yourself that it was precisely at those times when Jesus entered your life and was walking beside you?

There was that night I believed I would never get through...

There was that sickness from which I believed I would never recover...

There was that heartache I believed I could never endure...

There was that problem I believed I would never solve...

There was that cross I believed I could never bear...

And Jesus entered our lives.

We never noticed Him, because we were too busy with the noise.

We are not called merely to reciting prayers. We are called to intimacy with God... where heart speaks to heart.

You see... Jesus never left us.

He never left you and He never left me for one second, but we cannot hear His whispers to us unless we set aside time every day for silence.

EVERY DAY!

Now... undoubtably you will ask me, "What do I say to Him?"

How should I know...?

When you are in an intimate moment with someone you love, do you turn to someone else and ask, "What do I say?"

Perhaps we need such advice before conversing with strangers... before going into a job interview... but we should never need to say of our conversations with the Father, "I do not know what to say."

Try beginning with: I love you.

Try beginning with: I am afraid.

Would you like me to teach you a beautiful and powerful prayer?

I will say it for you, right this moment.

"Jesus."

That is all you need to say. Now... sit there and listen.

For the most part, God does not overpower us to enter our lives. Oh... sometimes He does... but even when He does He never destroys our will. God is not trying to sell us something. God is not trying to wedge His foot between our door and our door jamb. Jesus walks with us. And if we do not see Him, it is because we are not looking and we are not listening.

There is a line in today's Gospel reading that is so very important.

As they approached the village to which they were going, he gave the impression that he was going on farther.

He pretended to go on further. Why?

What was He waiting for?

An invitation.

How many times have we been asked if we were going to so and so's place, and responded by saying, "No. I was not invited."

The Lord does not crash parties either.

As they approached the village to which they were going, he gave the impression that he was going on farther. But they urged him, "Stay with us, for it is nearly evening and the day is almost over."

So he went in to stay with them. And it happened that, while he was with them at table, he took bread, said blessing, broke it, and gave it to them. With that their eyes were opened and they recognized him, but he vanished from their sight.

Why?

They did not need to see Him anymore.

Why?

They came to know that Jesus was still with them.

Fr. Lavalley

We believe in one Lord, Jesus Christ, the only Son of God, eternally begotten of the Father, God from God, Light from Light, true God from true God, begotten, not made, one in being with the Father...

Fourth Sunday of Easter

A reading from the Acts of the Apostles:

Then Peter stood up with the Eleven, raised his voice, and proclaimed, "Let the whole house of Israel know for certain that God has made both Lord and Christ, this Jesus whom you crucified."

Now when they heard this, they were cut to the heart, and they asked Peter and the other apostles, "What are we to do, my brothers?"

Peter said to them, "Repent and be baptized, every one of you, in the name of Jesus Christ for the forgiveness of your sins; and you will receive the gift of the Holy Spirit. For the promise is made to you and to your children and to all those far off, whomever the Lord our God will call."

He testified with many other arguments, and was exhorting them, "Save yourselves from this corrupt generation."

Those who accepted his message were baptized, and about three thousand persons were added that day.

A reading from the first Letter of Saint Peter:

Beloved: If you are patient when you suffer for doing what is good, this is grace before God. For to this you have been called, because Christ also suffered for you, leaving you an example that you should follow in his footsteps. He committed no sin, and no deceit was found in his mouth. When he was insulted, he returned no insult; when he suffered, he did not threaten; instead, he handed himself over to the one who judges justly. He himself bore our sins in his body upon the cross, so that, free from sin, we might live for righteousness. By his wounds you have been healed. For you had gone astray like sheep, but you have now returned to the shepherd and guardian of your souls.

A reading from the holy Gospel according to John:

Jesus said, "Amen, amen, I say to you, whoever does not enter a sheepfold through the gate, but climbs over elsewhere, is a thief and a robber. But whoever enters through the gate is the shepherd of the sheep. The gatekeeper opens it for him, and the sheep hear his voice, as the shepherd calls his own sheep by name and leads them out. When he has driven out all his own, he walks ahead of them, and the sheep follow him, because they recognize his voice. But they will not follow a stranger; they will run away from him, because they do not recognize the voice of strangers."

Although Jesus used this figure of speech, the Pharisees did not realize what he was trying to tell them. So Jesus said again, "Amen, amen, I say to you, I am the gate for the sheep. All who came before me are thieves and robbers, but the sheep did not listen to them. I am the gate. Whoever enters through me will be saved, and will come in and go out and find pasture. A thief comes only to steal and slaughter and destroy; I came so that they might have life and have it more abundantly."

If I possessed the grace and wisdom to take today's Scripture readings, consolidate them, and turn them into one small paragraph, my paragraph would read something like this:

Whatever you do, get to Jesus. The only thing in life that matters, when all is said and done, is that we go to Jesus, and that Jesus brings us to the Father.

We probably understood such theology more completely when we were children. I recall being exposed to some rather deep theology when I was in the first grade. In those days there existed a little book entitled *The Baltimore Catechism*. And while the book did not provide us with all of the answers we needed, it did provide us with a solid foundation upon which to build our spiritual life.

That little catechism book held us in good stead. It was filled with questions and answers. We were expected to memorize them.

The first question posed to us was this: Why did God make us?

The answer provided was: God made us to show forth His goodness and to share with us His everlasting happiness in Heaven.

For a six-year old that is some pretty profound theology. It is profound theology for a person of any age.

The second question posed to us was: What must we do to gain the happiness of Heaven?

And, the answer provided was: In order to gain the happiness of Heaven we must know, love, and serve God in this world.

Much later in life I discovered that a problem existed with the answer provided for that second question. The problem was that the answer did not challenge the reader further... and it should have.

You see... the problem with us is that we do not know God... completely. We do not love God... enough. We do not serve God... with all of our passion.

We need help.

And the help we need is not a formula... it is a person.

And the person from whom we need the help is Jesus Christ.

Jesus Christ delivers us to the Father.

What we have been given in Baptism is a wonderful gift. It is the gift of faith. But we have to open the eyes and ears of our soul in order to receive the gift of faith. God's grace exists for us... but we need to cooperate with His grace.

We need to cooperate.

We need to go to Jesus.

In today's Gospel reading, Jesus spoke to the Scribes and the Pharisees about the shepherd and the sheep. He speaks to us, today, about the shepherd and the sheep, yet we know He is not speaking about sheep at all.

What do we know about sheep?

Sheep are not overly intelligent. Sheep do not possess much in the way of defense mechanisms. Sheep do not have terrible teeth. Sheep do not have terrible claws. Sheep frighten easily.... sheep panic easily.... and when sheep become panicked and frightened they flock together.

And sometimes sheep stray...

So, with all of those things going against them, what do sheep have going for them?

Sheep have an innate ability to do one thing well. They can recognize the voice of the shepherd.

Sheep do not heed the voices of strangers. They do not heed the voices of marauders or robbers or thieves. Sheep will not follow anyone, but the shepherd... and that is an innate positive. Why?

Sheep absolutely need the shepherd... for without the shepherd terrible things will happen to them. They will stray. They will perish.

Most of us shudder at the thought of being compared to lowly sheep, but the Scriptural analogy of us as sheep exists for one very simple reason.

We behave very much like sheep.

And... would you like to know something else...?

We are not as intelligent as we think we are.

Most of us have been educated way beyond our level of intelligence... and we do not realize it.

We do not possess much in the way of defense mechanisms, either. We do not have terrible teeth. We do not have terrible claws. We panic easily... we frighten easily... and when we become panicked and frightened we flock together.

Quite frankly that is where we part company with sheep. Why?

Because we follow other voices.

We know the voice of the Shepherd is there, but sometimes we drown out His voice. And when we drown out His voice we hear other voices.

They begin as a whisper and magnify themselves until we can hear nothing else. Those voices have many different names. One is the voice of fear... one is the voice of despair. One is the voice of anger... one is the voice of hatred...   One is the voice of jealousy... and greed... and avarice... and lust... and intemperance... and selfishness.

Those voices can become rather loud, can they not?

So very loud...

There is another voice. It is the voice of the Shepherd. It is the voice of Jesus. And Jesus is saying:

"Listen to my voice."

"To lose me is to lose everything."

"To have me is to have everything."

Teresa of Avila, the little Carmelite nun who wrote her treatise... her guide to monastic life entitled *The Way of Perfection*... while kneeling on the floor at a ledge under a window, with no re-reading or editing, wrote: "God alone is sufficient."

What about the rest?

"God alone is sufficient."

Lord Jesus of the Eucharist, Divine Shepherd of our souls, help us to shut out the noise. Help us to hear only your voice and to follow it unconditionally.

Where do we turn to hear the voice of the Shepherd?

Where do we find the Shepherd?

Follow the light!

Fr. Lavalley

Through Him all things were made...

Fifth Sunday of Easter

A reading from the Acts of the Apostles:

As the number of disciples continued to grow, the Hellenists complained against the Hebrews because their widows were being neglected in the daily distribution. So the Twelve called together the community of the disciples and said, "It is not right for us to neglect the word of God to serve at table. Brothers, select from among you seven reputable men, filled with the Spirit and wisdom, whom we shall appoint to this task, whereas we shall devote ourselves to prayer and to the ministry of the word."

The proposal was acceptable to the whole community, so they chose Stephen, a man filled with faith and the Holy Spirit, also Philip, Prochorus, Nicanor, Timon, Parmenas, and Nicholas of Antioch, a convert to Judaism. They presented these men to the Apostles who prayed and laid hands on them. The word of God continued to spread, and the number of disciples in Jerusalem increased greatly; even a large group of priests were becoming obedient to the faith.

A reading from the first Letter of Saint Peter:

Beloved: Come to him, a living stone, rejected by human beings but chosen and precious in the sight of God, and, like living stones, let yourselves be built into a spiritual house to be a holy priesthood to offer spiritual sacrifices acceptable to God through Jesus Christ. For it says in Scripture: Behold, I am laying a stone in Zion, a cornerstone, chosen and precious, and whoever believes in it shall not be put to shame. Therefore, its value is for you who have faith, but for those without faith: "The stone that the builders rejected has become the cornerstone," and "A stone that will make people stumble, and a rock that will make them fall." They stumble by disobeying the word, as is their destiny.

You are "a chosen race, a royal priesthood, a holy nation, a people of his own, so that you may announce the praises" of him who called you out of darkness into his wonderful light.

A reading from the holy Gospel according to John:

Jesus said to his disciples: "Do not let your hearts be troubled. You have faith in God have also faith in me. In my Father's house there are many dwelling places. If there were not, would I have told you that I am going to prepare a place for you? And if I go and prepare a place for you, I will come back again and take you to myself, so that where I am you also may be. Where I am going you know the way."

Thomas said to him, "Master, we do not know where you are going; how can we know the way?"

Jesus said to him, "I am the way and the truth and the life. No one comes to the Father except through me. If you know me, then you will also know the Father. From now on you do know him and have seen him."

Philip said to him, "Master, show us the Father, and that will be enough for us."

Jesus said to him, "Have I been with you for so long a time and you still do not know me, Philip? Whoever has seen me has seen the Father. How can you say, 'Show us the Father'? Do you not believe that I am in the Father and the Father is in me? The words that I speak to you I do not speak on my own. The Father who dwells in me is doing his works. Believe me that I am in the Father and the Father is in me, or else, believe because of the works themselves. Amen, amen, I say to you, whoever believes in me will do the works that I do, and will do greater ones than these, because I am going to the Father."

Today's Scripture readings are absolutely wonderful, because they offer us much encouragement. What we are meant to learn from them is that it is alright not to be perfect. It is alright to be the pilgrim church. It is alright to be on our way.

Sometimes, I believe, when we look back upon the history of the Church we mistakenly observe that the zeal of the early converts was such that they could not wait to become food for the big cats in the coliseum. Our mistake is made in believing that they were all very perfect... kind of like Deborah Kerr in the movie *Quo Vadis*... where everything was perfect and holy- right down the line. Sometimes, I think, we are led to believe that back in the days of Caesar there were only three pious groups to which one could belong.

One could have been a virgin.... one could have been a martyr... or if one was really fortunate, one could have been a virgin-martyr. Again, sometimes, I believe, we get it into our heads that there was not much room for anything else... back then.

Ah... but all of a sudden our attention is drawn once again to the Acts of the Apostles... and the Acts of the Apostles describes for us situations that were quite different from those beliefs to which we so often ascribe.

In the Acts of the Apostles are found all kinds of people, upon whom it is our natural tendency to impose perfection and absolute holiness. Yet, a closer scrutiny of our reading reveals to us a group of people who are quarreling about who is getting the most food at the table. In one such instance the Greek converts were complaining that the widows of the Jewish converts were getting more than they were getting. They took their grievances to the Apostles, who, by the way, were given the monumental task of converting the world to Christianity, and complained about their portions of mashed potatoes.

The Apostles, of course, did the prudent thing; they passed the buck... and Deacons were created. Then, the Apostles levied upon the Deacons the authority to settle such disputes. What a cop out!

Instead of the perfection and holiness we are naturally disposed to assuming the early converts possessed... what is it that we actually find?

Pick, pick, pick. Petty, petty, petty.

Would you like me to open your eyes to something else... such pettiness is still around these days, is it not?

In reality, it is not the desert on the horizon of our lives that is the major contributor to our grievance and our dissatisfaction in life. No... more often than not it is that single grain of sand that slips into our shoe and irritates the sole of our foot as we walk along.

In the second reading of today's Scripture, Saint Peter addressed all of the pettiness by reminding us who we are. Peter said, "You are a holy nation. You are a royal priesthood. You are a people set apart. You belong to God. You are of Christ. Will you please stop your nonsense!"

"Grow up little Church."

"Grow up."

In today's reading of the holy Gospel according to Saint John, we are treated to some good news and some bad news. But, as is always the case in the Scripture, the good news out weighs the bad news. What is the bad news?

They did not get it.

The Apostles lived with Jesus. The Apostles broke bread with Jesus. The Apostles listened to Jesus morning, noon, and night... and still they did not get it. That was more than a little discouraging to Jesus.

At one point, Jesus enjoined the Apostles in a theological debate, whereupon, Jesus said to them, *"In my Father's house there are many dwelling places..."*

The Apostles asked, "How do we get there?"

Jesus replied, "You know the way. No one comes to the Father except through me. Do you not know that... by now?"

And they did not.

Thomas said to Him, *"Master, we do not know where you are going; how can we know the way?"*

"Thomas... *I am the way and the truth and the life."*

Philip joined in and said, "How can we know the way? We do not even know where you are going. *Master, show us the Father, and that will be enough for us...* just show us the Father."

Here is how I picture that entire exchange taking place:

I believe we become wrapped up in movie concepts of Jesus. The one that always portrays Him as being the teacher. He has everything but chalk in His hands and a blackboard at His back... and He is always standing in front of people who are gathered on the stony ground at His feet. All He needs is a blackboard and a piece of chalk.

To my mind, however, the conversation that Thomas and Philip had with Jesus sounds more like table talk.... not a classroom setting at all, but chairs around a dining room table or couches in the living room... not an auditorium, but a gathering around a breakfast table.

The good news is that Jesus never gave up on the Apostles... and He never gives up on you and me. If He has to explain it again to them... or us... one more time or two more times or three more times... He is going to keep at it until we get it right.

The Apostles said, *"Master, show us the Father..."*

Jesus responded by focusing them, not by lecturing them. Can you picture Him focusing Philip... taking Philip's face in His hands and looking him right in the eyes... patting his cheeks... and saying, "Aw Philip... don't you get it... don't you know me... look into my eyes... don't you get it, Phil?"

"Have I been with you for so long a time and you still do not know me, Philip?"

"Look into my eyes. You will see Him."

"Whoever has seen me has seen the Father."

Eventually, Thomas and Philip get it. Not right away, but they eventually get it, because of a wonderful gift soon to be bestowed upon mankind called: Pentecost.

Pentecost... when the Father and the Son bestow upon the Apostles a wonderful gift called the Holy Spirit. The same gift... the very same Holy Spirit... each one of us receives during Baptism.

This day would be a perfect day for each of us to sit in a quiet place and to reflect with Jesus on the life we have led thus far. And if we listen very carefully I am convinced we will hear Jesus asking us, "Did you not see me in this event in your life?"

"Did you not see me in that person who entered your life?"

"Did you not see me here... and there?"

"Do you not remember the time I carried you through that...?"

We do not even take the time to say thank-you... do we?

"Did you not see me...?"

"Did you not see me at the death of your father... at the death of your mother... at the death of your loved ones?"

"Did you not see me sitting beside the sick bed?"

"Did not you not see me in the birth of your child... in the life of your children?"

"Did you not see me in the baptism of your children?"

Look again.

Find Jesus.

"Truly, I say to you, as you did it to one of the least of these, my brothers, you did it to me."

"Truly, I say to you, as you did not do it to one of the least of these, you did not do it to me."

Where you find Jesus... you will find the Father.

And when we do not get it quite right... I believe... that is when Jesus loves us the most.

At those times when we are most dependent on Him... when we are lost... when we are confused... when we are sad... when we are without hope... let us not forget the words spoken by Jesus to His disciples for He speaks them to us.

Jesus said to his disciples, "Do not let your hearts be troubled..."

Fr. Lavalley

For us and for our salvation He came down from heaven: by the power of the Holy Spirit, He was born of the Virgin Mary, and became man...

Sixth Sunday of Easter

A reading from the Acts of the Apostles:

Philip went down to the city of Samaria and proclaimed the Christ to them. With one accord, the crowds paid attention to what was said by Philip when they heard it and saw the signs he was doing. For unclean spirits, crying out in a loud voice, came out of many possessed people, and many paralyzed or cripple people were cured. There was great joy in that city.

Now when the Apostles in Jerusalem heard that Samaria had accepted the word of God, they sent them Peter and John, who went down and prayed for them, that they might receive the Holy Spirit, for it had not yet fallen upon any of them; they had only been baptized in the name of the Lord Jesus. Then they laid hands on them and they received the Holy Spirit.

A reading from the first Letter of Saint Peter:

Beloved: Sanctify Christ as Lord in your hearts. Always be ready to give an explanation to anyone who asks you for a reason for your hope, but do it with gentleness and reverence, keeping your conscience clear, so that, when you are maligned, those who defame your good conduct in Christ may themselves be put to shame. For it is better to suffer for doing good, if that be the will of God, than for doing evil.

For Christ also suffered for sins once, the righteous for the sake of the unrighteous, that he might lead you to God. Put to death in the flesh, he was brought to life in the spirit.

A reading from the holy Gospel according to John:

Jesus said to his disciples, "If you love me, you will keep my commandments. And I will ask the Father, and he will give you another Advocate to be with you always, the Spirit of truth, whom the world cannot accept, because it neither sees nor knows him. But you know him, because he remains with you, and will be in you. I will not leave you orphans; I will come to you. In a little while the world will no longer see me, but you will see me, because I live and you will live. On that day you will realize that I am in the Father and you are in me and I in you. Whoever has my commandments and observes them is the one who loves me. And whoever loves me will be loved by my Father, and I will love him and reveal myself to him."

This day is the sixth Sunday of Easter and we continue to prepare ourselves for the great feast of Pentecost. Throughout the Easter season, this season of new light, we are called to be Easter people; to be God's holy people.

Today, I am going to talk about you... about yourselves as parishioners of Saint Francis Xavier and about my reasons for coming to Saint Francis... why I consider Saint Francis Xavier to be my parish.

Several years ago, due to a multitude of age-related ailments, I resigned from the parish to which I had been assigned. What followed was a very strange time for me and I was left feeling very disorientated, especially on the weekends. I thought to myself, "What do I do, now?" and "Who am I?"

For many, many years I celebrated every Sunday mass... every feast day... and every holy day with the people of my parish. All of a sudden my life changed. I decided I needed to find a new place of worship, so I began attending services here at Saint Francis Xavier, with you. My primary reason for attending Saint Francis Xavier, in the beginning, was due to the fact that Father Lavalley is my best friend and I knew his parish would be a comfortable place of worship. Since I began attending Saint Francis Xavier, however, my motivation for returning to Father Lavalley's parish has changed. My friendship with Father Lavalley has not changed, but my motivation for remaining in his parish has changed. I come here now because of you and because of what I experience in this parish.

I watch you.

Usually I am seated in Sanctuary, to the right of the altar, and I miss very little. I have watched you during the Sundays of our liturgical celebration and I never fail to be moved by your reverence for our Lord and Savior Jesus Christ. During Holy Week, however, I was particularly stirred by your participation and your reverence. On Good Friday, when you came down, in two lines, to reverence the Cross... the symbol of our salvation... the symbol of our faith... I watched your faces and observed that your countenance was a living sign of who you are. You are God's people. You know that... and you live that.

Every Sunday, after attending mass at Saint Francis Xavier, I depart feeling nourished. I depart feeling as though I have been fed. And the reason for this is because of the atmosphere of this parish and the faith of this people... You!

Whenever people, who have not attended mass regularly or who have not attended mass for a long while, confide in me that they do not know where to go to attend mass, because they do not know where they will fit in or because they do not know where they will feel comfortable... I tell them, "I have just the place for you."

"Go to Saint Francis Xavier," I say. "You will feel right at home... and you will feel right at home because of the people who are there; because of the pastor who is there."

There are many reasons why we feel right at home in this place. In part it is because of the way things are done at Saint Francis Xavier. The liturgies are performed well. The choir is an excellent choir. The pastor is an excellent homilist; he teaches, inspires, and builds. All of those things are what we refer to as being a witness.

Saint Francis Xavier is the proverbial beacon of hope... that shining light... that city on the hill. One can pick out Saint Francis Xavier from just about everywhere. Everywhere one travels in the neighborhoods of Burlington, Colchester, and Winooski, one can spot the towers of Saint Francis. The towers of Saint Francis Xavier are a sign to the rest of the community... not only a sign to the residents of Chittenden County... but a sign to many people traveling to Vermont or through Vermont that this is a place of holiness... a place of peace... a place of worship.

Signs are what Jesus talked to His disciples about in today's Gospel reading. He spoke about being "that" sign... being "that" witness. Very simply... Jesus said, *"If you love me you will keep my commandments."*

By loving one another... as you do... by caring for one another... as you do... through your commitment to your parish you are a sign to one another, and to those whom you touch throughout your daily lives, that God is indeed present in this place. There is faith here. You believe in what you are doing.

Saint Peter said, *"Sanctify Christ as Lord in your hearts."*

Make a holy place for Christ.

Always be ready to give an explanation to anyone who asks you for a reason for your hope...

Often we do not need to do those things with words. Our actions can speak volumes. People can sense holiness.

Why is the parish of Saint Francis Xavier so special?

There is something going on within this parish that is very good and very holy. Persons not of this parish sense such things when they come to visit you. And, it is not uncommon for persons not of this parish to return to this parish to continue to celebrate Christ with you after what they thought would only be a one time event.

That is what is referred to as giving witness. That is what is meant by living the commandments. That is what is meant by loving God. That is what is meant by loving one another. That is the sign of the Christian church.

Saint Peter provided us with a guide for witnessing to those not of our faith by telling us to do so with gentleness and reverence.

I have never felt put upon during my association with the parishioners of Saint Francis Xavier. There is a gentleness and a peacefulness that exists in this parish. So... if people criticize you for being Catholic... for living as you are... good! Were you to be criticized by people not of this parish, I suspect, it would be because they sense something within you... they sense something here... they sense something that makes them desirous of possessing the feeling that shines from within each of you. Such is human nature.

We are called to be that light... that shining city on the hill... to be that beacon shining in the dark... to be that loving presence in our world. The only hands and voice Jesus has today are the ones we give Him. We are the ones who reach out and touch others in the name of the Lord. We are the ones who speak comforting words to others... kind words... supportive words. We are the ones who are there to tell others the good news- *No matter what happens everything will be good, because God loves us and we love God.*

As we move closer to the great feast of Pentecost... a celebration of the coming of the Holy Spirit... we are reminded that the Holy Spirit is already here. The Holy Spirit moves among us.

Pentecost is a celebration of renewal... a celebration of the Holy Spirit moving upon the face of the world. We live with that Holy Spirit. You and I could not do what we are doing if we did not possess the Holy Spirit. You could not put on a show of faith... such as you do... for it would not be real. However, with the Holy Spirit moving upon our lives and working within us... feeding us... guiding us... teaching us... inspiring us... giving us courage to go forth... the faith you project is real. Our faith is of the Holy Spirit. It is God's spirit working within us.

Pentecost is a celebration of God's spirit working within each and every one of us. It is a reminder that we are called to new life. We celebrate new life during our Easter observance and with Pentecost comes the big celebration of the Church. Yet, while we designate this time to celebrate the Holy Spirit moving upon our lives and upon our world, in reality, this is something that we do day in and day out... something that we should do day in and day out.

Occasionally, I attend Saint Francis Xavier during the weekday for morning mass. Truthfully, I am awestruck by how many of you attend morning mass during the weekday. There is not just a handful of parishioners attending mass at Saint Francis on weekday mornings. The church is not an empty church. Dare I say that approximately half of the Saint Francis Xavier Sunday morning congregation can be found at Saint Francis most weekday mornings. At other Catholic parishes, with which I am familiar, one could count on one hand the number of regular weekday morning mass attendees, but not here. Why?

Simply stated... you are living your faith.

Please do not misconstrue my words or my intent for saying so. I am not passing judgement upon Christians of other parishes or people of other faiths. All will do as their consciences dictate. I speak of my observations because those are the things that I see here... because these are the reasons for my hope: I see God working here... through you; I see a living Church; I see that no matter what is closed, sold, bartered or bought... the Church goes on... because it is God's church.

Popes will come and popes will go. Bishops will come and bishops will go. The people of God will remain. We are the Church. It is very important for us to take the time to reflect on who we are.

So... as the visitor from outside... as one who sits on the side... I wanted to take this opportunity to speak to you of such things. I wanted you to know how very important it is for us to know who we are... what our faith is... and to take the knowledge of those two things to heart. Such observations are not made to pat ourselves on the back or to swell our heads with foolish pride. Very simply... such observations are made so that we can give thanks to God for who we are... and for what God is doing in our lives.

Such is the witness of Easter.

Such is the witness of Pentecost.

Such is the witness of what the Church is to be in all the world.

If you want to know what a people are really like... watch them when they pray.

Fr. Ragis

For our sake He was crucified under Pontius Pilate; He suffered, died, and was buried...

Ascension of the Lord

A reading from the Acts of the Apostles:

In the first book, Theophilus, I dealt with all that Jesus did and taught until the day he was taken up, after giving instructions through the Holy Spirit to the Apostles whom he had chosen. He presented himself alive to them by many proofs after he had suffered, appearing to them during forty days and speaking about the kingdom of God. While meeting with them, he enjoined them not to depart from Jerusalem, but to wait for "the promise of the Father about which you have heard me speak; for John baptized me with water, but in a few days you will be baptized with the Holy Spirit."

When they had gathered together they asked him, "Lord, are you at this time going to restore the kingdom to Israel?"

He answered them, "it is not for you to know the times or the seasons that the Father has established by his own authority. But you will receive power when the Holy Spirit comes upon you, and you will be my witnesses in Jerusalem, throughout Judea and Samaria, and to the ends of the earth."

When he had said this, as they were looking on, he was lifted up, and a cloud took him from their sight. While they were looking intently at the sky as he was going, suddenly two men dressed in white garments stood beside them. They said, "Men of Galilee, why are you standing there looking at the sky? This Jesus who has been taken up from you into heaven will return in the same way as you have seen him going to heaven."

A reading from the Letter of Saint Paul to the Ephesians:

Brothers and sisters: May the God of our Lord Jesus Christ, the Father of glory, give you a Spirit of wisdom and revelation resulting in the knowledge of him. May the eyes of your hearts be enlightened, that you may know what is the hope that belongs to his call, what are the riches of glory in his inheritance among the holy ones, and what is the surpassing greatness of his power for us who believe, in accord with the exercise of his great might, which he worked in Christ, raising him from the dead and seating him at his right hand in the heavens, far above every principality, authority, power, and dominion, and every name that is named not only in this age but also in the one to come. And he put all things beneath his feet and gave him as head over all things to the church, which is his body, the fullness of the one who fills all things in every way.

A reading from the holy Gospel according to Matthew:

The eleven disciples went to Galilee, to the mountain to which Jesus had ordered them. When they saw him, they worshiped, but they doubted. Then Jesus approached and said to them, "All power in heaven and on earth has been given to me. Go, therefore, and make disciples of all nations, baptizing them in the name of the Father, and of the Son, and of the Holy Spirit, teaching them to observe all that I have commanded you. And behold, I am with you always, until the end of the age."

During Holy Week we embarked on a journey. It was a journey of faith and of trust and of hope. Our journey continues. It does not end on this day, the Ascension of the Lord, but our Easter journey... the Paschal mystery... has brought us to a tremendous event that we cannot pass by without looking at it and asking, "What does it all mean?"

What is this all about?

Is it good-bye?

Is it farewell?

What is it?

Let us take a look at the mystery of the Ascension.

Observed from a perfectly human point of view we find a group of people dejected and downhearted. They are called the Apostles. They had been on a roller coaster ride. Their roller coaster ride actually lasted for about three years. And just when they thought they knew what God's plan was... Jesus told them it was not.

Right down the line Jesus had been teaching and teaching and teaching... and the Apostles still did not get it. Jesus makes this point to us through Philip, to whom He said, *"Have I been with you for so long a time and you still do not know me, Philip?"*

"You still do not get it, Philip... do you?"

Then... the event of the Holy Eucharist came to pass and everything looked fine... until the event of the Holy Eucharist was followed by the event of the Crucifixion... and the Crucifixion was followed by the death and the burial of Jesus.

Once again, the hearts of the Apostles were broken.

Next came the glorious Resurrection and the Apostles found Jesus walking in the glory of His Easter morn, and everything was fine, once more. But Jesus did not return to them in the manner with which the

Apostles were familiar. His business was not business as usual. It was anything but business as usual. Jesus was there... Jesus was not there. Jesus was in their presence... but they could not see Him.

Eventually they would see Him, but it would take the gift of something else for the Apostles to see Jesus. It would take the gift of faith... a gift from the Father.

Only those who believe are able to see.

Jesus returned, and His salutation became, *"Shalom Aleichem: May peace be upon you."*

"Not peace as the world gives it. As I give it to you."

Jesus was among them and He made it very clear to the Apostles that, in some ways, He was the same Jesus they knew. He went out into boats with them. He went to the lake with them. He even cooked breakfast on the beach for them. He cooked fish for them and He ate with them.

The Apostles saw all of those wonderful things and they rejoiced, but Jesus said to them, "I am not staying."

"I am not staying, but I am sending someone to you... but for that someone to come, I need to leave."

Jesus used another word to describe the one who would follow: the Paraclete.

Is that not a strange word for God... the Paraclete?

The Paraclete... it means "the defense attorney", the One who will plead our case. It means the Holy Spirit.

"I will send Him, but I have to go first."

The Apostles did not understand any of what Jesus had told them, yet despite their lack of understanding... He went up, up, up and away. Why did Jesus leave them?

He did not.

He did not leave them. To see Him they will just have to see Him in another way. Corporally, yes... Jesus went to Heaven, but He left the Eucharist. Why did He go to Heaven?

Because Heaven is home.

Why is it home?

Because that is where the Father lives.

Heaven was always home to Jesus. It was always home... and one should always want to go home.

Our story does not end there, however.

Jesus did not want to exist as an only child.

There is a wonderful word that we are challenged not to exclude from our celebration this day: Home.

"Go, therefore, and make disciples of all nations, baptizing them in the name of the Father, and of the Son, and of the Holy Spirit, teaching them to observe all that I have commanded you. And, behold, I am with you always, until the end of the age."

Jesus left home... Heaven. Jesus went back home... Heaven. And when you and I contemplate Heaven through the event of Baptism, we can say "home" when we speak of Heaven.

Go home.

Heaven is what we were made for... and that is the mystery of the Ascension of the Lord. Heaven is Jesus' home. It is our home, too!

"I am the vine. You are the branches."

This day we celebrate Jesus' homecoming... and ours.

The Holy Spirit is the next gift.

Fr. Lavalley

Seventh Sunday of Easter

A reading from the Acts of the Apostles:

After Jesus had been taken up to heaven the Apostles returned to Jerusalem from the mount called Olivet, which is near Jerusalem, a Sabbath day's journey away.

When they entered the city they went to the upper room where they were staying, Peter and John and James and Andrew, Philip and Thomas, Bartholomew and Matthew, James son of Alphaeus, Simon the Zealot, and Judas son of James. All these devoted themselves with one accord to prayer, together with some women, and Mary the mother of Jesus, and his brothers.

A reading from the first Letter of Saint Peter:

Beloved: Rejoice to the extent that you share in the sufferings of Christ, so that when his glory is revealed you may also rejoice exultantly. If you are insulted for the name of Christ, blessed are you, for the Spirit of glory and of God rests upon you. But let no one among you be made to suffer as a murderer, a thief, an evildoer, or as an intriguer. But whoever is made to suffer as a Christian should not be ashamed but glorify God because of the name.

A reading from the holy Gospel according to John:

Jesus raised his eyes to heaven and said, "Father, the hour has come. Give glory to your son, so that your son may glorify you, just as you gave him authority over all people, so that your son may give eternal life to all you gave him. Now this is eternal life, that they should know you, the only true God, and the one whom you sent, Jesus Christ. I glorified you on earth by accomplishing the work you gave me to do. Now glorify me, Father, with you, with the glory that I had with you before the world began."

"I revealed your name to those whom you gave me out of the world. They belonged to you, and you gave them to me, and they have kept your word. Now they know that everything you gave me is from you, because the words you gave to me I have given to them, and they accepted them and truly understood that I came from you, and they have believed that you sent me. I pray for them. I do not pray for the world but for the ones you have given me, because they are yours, and everything of mine is yours and everything of yours is mine, and I have been glorified in them. And now I will no longer be in the world, but they are in the world, while I am coming to you.

Jesus said, *"I pray for them."*

To be prayed for by Jesus... why?

No one has taken you more seriously than our Savior.

No one in your entire life has been more serious about you than has Jesus Christ.

No one has wanted what was best for you more than the Lord.

He prayed for us...

That was not an event that took place one day. Through Him... with Him... and in Him... He prays for us today at mass.

Why?

He tells us why.

Because we are so precious to the Father.

Do you recall what it was like the first time you held a baby in your arms?

Do you recall how awkward you felt?

Do you recall how you were more than a little frightened that you might drop the precious bundle you were holding in your arms?

Jesus' prayer for us... to the Father... is akin to holding a newborn child in your arms in that Jesus is saying to the Father, "Here, I want you to take care of them."

To be in the hands of Jesus... it is a good place to be.

What a wonderfully secure place...

Jesus prays for us because He takes His role seriously and knows that He serves us best by praying for us.

His is an example we would do well to emulate... and, to that end, what we really need to do is to spend more time praying for one another. If we would spend half as much time praying for one another as we do worrying about one another, can you imagine how much better off we all would be?

f we would spend more time praying for one another, instead of manipulating one another or trying to change one another's life, can you imagine how much better off we all would be?

If we would only come to the realization that we really do not know what is best for one another, but that God does... and, so knowing, we would take our concerns and cares to the feet of God, can you imagine how much better off we all would be?

And... in praying... we would not pray for one another to do our will... but for one another to find God, can you imagine how much better off we all would be?

What we need to pray for is for people to find God; not according to our plan... but according to God's plan.

Not according to our plan... but according to God's plan!

Jesus prays for us because our's is an uphill battle. Life is like a treadmill. Yet, we should rejoice to the extent that we share in the sufferings of Christ.

Part of our Christian journey is the Cross. We should never be surprised nor discouraged when we are asked to carry a cross. When we are made to carry a cross or are asked to bear the burden of the cross in those moments we are brought closer to Christ.

I always get the goose bumps when I read today's passage from the Acts of the Apostles, because I am mindful of the location of the Ascension of our Lord. As Yogi Berra was fond of saying, "It's deja vu all over again."

After Jesus had been taken up to heaven, the Apostles returned to Jerusalem from the mount called Olivet...

It is the Agony in the Garden.

It is the very same spot.

The location of the Ascension of our Lord, and the scene of Christ's suffering are one and the same.

Jesus took His disciples back to the scene of His suffering. He took them back to the place where He sweated blood. He took them back to the place of Judas' kiss... to Peter's sword... to the ear that was cut off by

Peter's sword. He took them back into the darkness to show them His light.

... the Apostles returned to Jerusalem from the mount called Olivet...

All of a sudden the sun shined.

We need to develop a new or a greater devotion to the Ascension of our Lord, because... as the Apostles did... we are going to find ourselves on Olivet, and sometimes it will be dark, and sometimes it will be light... and we will have our own crosses to bear.

It is easy to forget that the cross makes us strong. The cross gives us strength. It is difficult to realize such things during the worst of times... but hard times make us strong. We need to embrace our struggles. We need to thank God for them.

One Sunday morning the congregation of an unnamed parish gathered to celebrate mass. Just as the mass was about to begin, Satan appeared. He appeared as fierce and as ferocious as you could possibly imagine. The congregation panicked and people began fleeing from the church. The parishioners were terrified and they ran screaming and hollering from the church. Everyone ran... except for one little old man.

One little old man knelt in the pew with his rosary in his hands... his head was bowed in prayer.

Satan stomped over to where the little old man was kneeling and roared, "Do you know who I am?"

The little old man looked up from his rosary and replied, "Yup."

Satan, looking somewhat incredulous at such a response, asked, "You do?"

"Yup. Sure do," the little old man replied.

"Are you afraid of me?"

"Nope."

"You're not...?"

"Nope," replied the little old man.

"Do you know I can hurt you?" asked Satan.

"Yup," answered the little old man.

"Do you know I can terrorize you?" asked Satan.

"Uh huh," responded the little old man.

"Do you know I can do things to you... horrible things... that are beyond your ability to comprehend?" asked Satan.

"Yes I do," replied the little old man.

"And, you are still not afraid of me?" asked Satan.

"Nope."

"Why not?"

The little old man looked up at Satan and said, "Why would I be afraid of you... for sixty-two years I've been married to your sister!"

For my readers who are of the female persuasion please replace the little old man in our story with a little old lady... and give Satan a brother...

Our crosses make us strong. They give us courage.

Let us consider the Apostles... on the mount called Olivet. When Jesus ascended to Heaven they were left all alone. They did not have the Holy Spirit, yet. The Holy Spirit was en route, but the Apostles did not know that.

Jesus was gone... and the Apostles did not possess a five year plan, or even a five day plan. They did not have time to formulate even a five hour plan. They did not have statistics... they did not even have a flash-light... they did not have a clue. They did not have anything... or did they?

In today's reading from the Acts of the Apostles, the author carefully scribed the names of the Apostles gathered on Olivet that day. Why did not the author simply write "the Eleven" and leave it at that?

No... the author wrote *...Peter and John and James and Andrew, Philip and Thomas, Bartholomew and Matthew, James son of Alphaeus, Simon the Zealot, and Judas son of James.* Why?

Because they possessed a grace. Even before the Holy Spirit de-scended upon them, they possessed a grace. Would you hazard a guess as to what that grace was?

They had each other.

Sometimes we pray for the grace of God, and we look up, and we do not believe we have been heard, let alone answered. That is because the answers we receive are not always up... sometimes they are down... sometimes they are vertical to us... and sometimes the answer is stand-ing beside us. Sometimes the answer is a person that God sends to us for that moment. And the person God sends to us in such moments possesses something that grace alone does not have: legs and feet upon which to walk toward us; hands and arms with which to hold us; eyes that look into our eyes; ears with which to hear us; and lips upon which a consoling word can be uttered.

Take a moment to recall all of the people who appeared beside you during your moments of trial and tribulation... people whom God had sent to you.

When I look back on my life I can revisit troubling times and recall with ease this person or that person who sat beside me... who held my hand... who held me in comforting arms. At the time it might not have seemed as much at all... but it was enough.

It was enough.

God gives us grace in people.   Sometimes we take such things for granted, but it is our duty to cherish the grace of those people who help us to walk along the way... to cherish the grace of the people who set the example for us... to cherish the grace of the people who love us.

And one thing more...

All these devoted themselves with one accord to prayer, together with some women, and Mary the mother of Jesus...

We will always have our Lady.

Fr. Lavalley

On the third day He rose again in fulfillment of the Scriptures; He ascended into heaven and is seated at the right hand of the Father...

Vigil of Pentecost

A reading from the Book of Genesis:

The whole world spoke the same language, using the same words. While the people were migrating in the east, they came upon a valley in the land of Shinar and settled there. They said to one another, "Come, let us mold bricks and harden them with fire." They used bricks for stone, and bitumen for mortar. Then they said, "Come, let us build ourselves a city and a tower with its top in the sky, and so make a name for ourselves; otherwise we shall be scattered all over the earth."

The Lord came down to see the city and the tower that the people had built. Then the Lord said, "If now, while they are one people, all speaking the same language, they have started to do this, nothing will later stop them from doing whatever they presume to do. Let us then go down there and confuse their language, so that one will not understand what another says."

Thus the Lord scattered them from there all over the earth, and they stopped building the city. That is why it was called Babel, because there the Lord confused the speech of all the world. It was from that place that he scattered them all over the earth.

A reading from the Letter of Saint Paul to the Romans:

Brothers and sisters: We know that all creation is groaning in labor pains even until now; and not only that, but we ourselves, who have the first fruits of the Spirit, we also groan within ourselves as we wait for adoption, the redemption of our bodies. For in hope we were saved. Now hope that sees is not hope. For who hopes for what one sees? But if we hope for what we do not see, we wait with endurance.

In the same way, the Spirit too comes to the aid of our weakness; for we do not know how to pray as we ought, but the Spirit himself intercedes with inexpressible groanings. And the one who searches hearts knows what is the intention of the spirit, because he intercedes for the holy ones according to God's will.

A reading from the holy Gospel according to John:

On the last and greatest day of the feast, Jesus stood up and exclaimed, "Let anyone who thirsts come to me and drink. As Scripture says: Rivers of living water will flow from within him who believes in me."

He said this in reference to the Spirit that those who came to believe in him were to receive. There was, of course, no Spirit yet, because Jesus had not yet been glorified.

This day draws us one day closer to the great feast of Pentecost, which is the culmination of the Easter season that began on Holy Thursday. During the past fifty-two days we have been reflecting on segments of this great event. The entire period forms one event called the Paschal Mystery.

The Paschal Mystery is the dying and rising of Jesus Christ to new life, and the outpouring of the Spirit. Through the waters of Baptism and the outpouring of the Spirit we are born to new life. We are called to that new life.

As a child educated in the Catholic school system, whenever I pictured receiving the Holy Spirit I formed an image in my head of a bottle... a big milk bottle... and when I was filled with Grace, I pictured that bottle being filled. Whenever I sinned, however, I imagined the contents of that bottle being greatly diminished. Where the contents of the bottle went... I did not know... I did not give it that much thought... but my concept of receiving Grace was one, whereby, my hands were raised above my head, forming a funnel, and the Holy Spirit poured Itself into my soul... a soul that was for me... a milk bottle.

Inevitably, I grew up and discovered, soon enough, that receiving the Holy Spirit was more involved than the image I had created as a grade-schooler.

As I began to study Scripture, I became acutely aware of one word: baptize. Generally speaking... when you and I think of Baptism, we think of it in terms of our personal and physical experience. For most of us this means water being poured very carefully on the foreheads of our babies so that they do not get too wet and too fussy.

The meaning of the Greek word "baptizer" is to be totally surrounded by water. Not unlike our first nine months of life, the Greek concept of Baptism was to be completely immersed in waters of new life. The symbolism, therefore, is not that I am taking God's life into me... into my milk bottle as I once imagined... but that I am being brought into God's life. Thus... receiving the Holy Spirit means that we are being brought into the life of God. The life of God... the power of the Holy Spirit... surrounds us entirely. We are totally immersed in the Spirit of God.

We will discover in our Gospel readings for Pentecost Sunday, that Jesus went to His disciples and found their doors were locked. Their doors were locked out of fear. Jesus passed through their locked doors, however, and said to them, "Peace."

You and I will have experiences similar to those of the disciples, cowering behind their locked doors, many times in our lives. We lock our doors out of fear.

Now... the doors to which I am referring are not the doors of our office buildings or the doors of our homes. No... I am speaking about the doors of our selves.

There are times in our lives when we attempt to lock out God. We attempt to bar the door to God, because we are not sure of what He will do to us... and we believe we will be safer if we keep our distance from Him. Yet, the very essence of God... of being in life with Jesus Christ and the Holy Spirit... means that no door is locked. There is no protection from the essence of God in our lives. We are brought completely into His life.

Again... as we will discover in our readings for Pentecost Sunday, the disciples of Christ will be found cowering behind locked doors, and the spirit of God will descend upon them as a mighty wind and fire. He will blow open their doors. Whether they like it or not, the disciples will be so caught up in power of God, that they will find themselves in the last place they wanted to be. They will be no longer safe. They will be no longer be hidden. Despite their predilections to the contrary, they will publicly proclaim the wonderful things God has done and the wonderful things God can do. Everyone who will hear the witness of Christ's disciples will be completely amazed and enthralled by what they are hearing.

Not coincidentally, Pentecost took place during the height of the Jewish holiday, Shavuot. Because of this, Jews gathered in Jerusalem from all corners of the Mediterranean. They went to Jerusalem on pilgrimage and a veritable potpourri of languages were spoken there. Yet, the disciples spoke to all of them, each in their own language.

"How can that be?" the pilgrims proclaimed. "Something fantastic is taking place."

Were we to read further into the Acts of the Apostles, we would come to know that, as a result of the workings of the Holy Spirit, five-thousand people were added to the one hundred and twenty contemporary followers of Jesus Christ. Those converts were made, not by the works of the Apostles, but by God touching them and by God drawing them into this new life.

It would not surprise me at all if, at some point in the future, scientists are able to isolate a Catholic gene existing in all followers of Jesus Christ. It has been my experience that even those persons, who identify themselves as Christians but do not attend church services, and those persons, who say they have no use for the Church, still identify themselves as Catholics when asked to which denomination they belong. I believe such a gene exists within our very bones and fiber. It is not unlike the Spirit that dwelled within the Apostles... the one that compelled the Apostles to proclaim publicly, and while on trial in various Roman courts, "We are not able **not** to speak out!"

As a consequence of being brought into God's life we are not able **not** to be Catholic. Whether we like all of the ceremony and ritual associated with our faith... or not. We are who we are and we know who we are. It is a part of our identity.

The feast of the coming Pentecost goes on and on. It is not a thing of the past. The same Spirit moves upon us, today... as It moved upon the Apostles in the beginning. It is the same Spirit at work in the Church, today... as It was in the beginning.

When God touches your life... when you open your heart to Jesus Christ and the Holy Spirit... changes occur within you for which you have absolutely no explanation. Yet, you are instantly aware of a marvelous feeling that comes upon you. A wonderful glow comes upon you. It is difficult to explain this feeling to persons who have not opened their hearts to God... who have not opened their hearts to Jesus Christ... who have not opened their hearts to the Holy Spirit. But... you will know when you have been touched by God.

One of the most difficult reconciliations we face as Christians... as Catholics... as passionate believers in the Most Holy Trinity, is this: The glow fades, but the power remains.

The glow fades, but the power remains.

Do not mistake the glow for the power. One thing that happens to people of faith... as we journey forth... is there are times when prayer and being followers of Jesus Christ can become as exciting as sitting around and watching paint dry. At times we are inclined to feel as though we are not getting anything out of our faith... out of our devotion to our Lord and Savior Jesus Christ. The glow has faded.

The glow fades, but the power remains.

The gift of the Holy Spirit remains in each of our souls. The Holy Spirit continues to work in each of our lives. It is our responsibility to use the gifts God has given to us. We do not need to seek external forces to influence our lives and the lives of those with whom we touch. The gifts God has given to us dwell within. They are who we are.

Be who you are.

Saint Paul wrote the following words of encouragement to Timothy, a young priest, at a time when Timothy was having a hard time ministering to the people of Ephesus. *"For this reason I remind you to fan into flame the gift of God, which is in you through the laying on of my hands, for God gave us a spirit not of fear but of power and love and self-control."*

The gift of God is within you. The gift of God of which Saint Paul spoke is the Spirit that entered into you by the laying on of hands at Baptism and at Confirmation.

Saint Paul impressed upon Timothy that the Holy Spirit did not want him to be afraid of people, but to be wise and strong and to love the people of Ephesus; to enjoy being with them. He admonished Timothy to stir up his inner power, and so doing, "...you will never be afraid to tell others about the Lord."

A few lines further in Saint Paul's second letter to Timothy, Saint Paul counseled Timothy to *"...guard the good deposit entrusted to you."*

Once again... the gift of which Saint Paul spoke is a gift that is given to every one of us. And while we may occasionally forget that the gift dwells within us... or we consciously set the gift aside... it is incumbent upon us to use the gift given to us by God, through the Holy Spirit. We need to rekindle, or fan into flame, the gift of God. We need to live and work in the power of God's Holy Spirit, because that is what makes us the Church.

So, the great feast of Pentecost is upon us. From Pentecost until Advent we are going to reflect and meditate on how to live this Paschal mystery. Beginning with Easter Sunday and ending with Pentecost we will have celebrated this great event... an event central to our Christian faith. For the remaining Sundays... which we call Ordinary Time... we will reflect on all of the different aspects of being followers of Jesus. But let us never forget the essentials:

God's spirit has brought us into His own life.

The glow may fade, but the power remains.

Do not mistake the glow... for the power.

Fr. Ragis

Pentecost Sunday

A reading from the Acts of the Apostles:

When the time for Pentecost was fulfilled, they were all in one place together. And suddenly there came from the sky a noise like a strong driving wind, and it filled the entire house in which they were. Then there appeared to them tongues as of fire, which parted and came to rest on each one of them. And they were all filled with the Holy Spirit and began to speak in different tongues, as the Spirit enabled them to proclaim.

Now there were devout Jews from every nation under heaven staying in Jerusalem. At this sound, they gathered in a large crowd, but they were confused because each one heard them speaking in his own language. They were astounded, and in amazement they asked, "Are not all these people who are speaking Galileans? Then how does each of us hear them in his native language? We are Parthians, Medes, and Elamites, inhabitants of Mesopotamia, Judea and Cappadocia, Pontus and Asia, Phrygia and Pamphylia, Egypt and the districts of Libya near Cyrene, as well as travelers from Rome, both Jews and converts to Judaism, Cretans and Arabs, yet we hear them speaking in our own tongues of the mighty acts of God."

A reading from the first Letter of Saint Paul to the Corinthians:

Brothers and sisters: No one can say, "Jesus is Lord," except by the Holy Spirit.

There are different kinds of spiritual gifts but the same Spirit; there are different forms of service but the same Lord; there are different workings but the same God who produces all of them in everyone. To each individual the manifestation of the Spirit is given for some benefit.

As a body is one though it has many parts, and all the parts of the body, though many, are one body, so also Christ. For in one Spirit we were all baptized into one body, whether Jews or Greeks, slaves or free persons, and we were all given to drink of one Spirit.

A reading from the holy Gospel according to John:

On the evening of that first day of the week, when the doors were locked, where the disciples were, for fear of the Jews, Jesus came and stood in their midst and said to them, "Peace be with you." When he had said this, he showed them his hands and his side. The disciples rejoiced when they saw the Lord. Jesus said to them again, "Peace be with you. As the Father has sent me, so I send you." And when he had said this, he breathed on them and said to them, "Receive the Holy Spirit. Whose sins you forgive are forgiven them, and whose sins you retain are retained."

This day is Pentecost Sunday... and we begin the great feast of the Pentecost by praying, "Come Holy Spirit." That is a beautiful prayer provided we realize this one thing: the coming of the Holy Spirit is not a future event. The Holy Spirit has been active in the world from the very beginning. From the dawn of Creation the Spirit of God breathed over the chaos and the world as it was. The Spirit of God breathed life... and human life came to be.

Throughout our readings of the sacred history... the Holy Scripture... we witness the activity of the Holy Spirit from the very beginning. There is not a page within the story of human history upon which the Holy Spirit has not moved.

Today, let us take a look at a couple of wonderful events... events during which the Spirit of God surprised us by doing things that seemed absolutely impossible.

Perhaps the most obvious of these events is contained in today's first reading of the Gospel. Therein, we encounter a little band of people, Apostles, who had no direction... no courage... no clue as to where to go or what to do... and they were groping for answers, together. Yet, out of that little band of people rose the Church. And it was so because the Spirit of God moved upon them.

There are wonderful examples in the sacred Scripture of the Spirit of God... the breath of God... doing things we cannot even imagine as being possible. Elijah the Prophet was preparing to die and it appeared as though his passing would mark the end of an era until his young pupil Elisha said, *"Please let there be a double portion of your spirit upon me."*

And the new spirit of Elijah was upon the land. That "new spirit" was the Holy Spirit working.

Perhaps one of the most beautiful examples of the Holy Spirit pro-vided to us in the Old Testament is found in the story of the dry bones. What are they?

They are dead men's bones.

Will they come alive again?

"Son of man, can these bones live?"

If you say so...

"Behold, I will cause breath to enter you, and you shall live."

The Spirit of God.

The Spirit of God... the Holy Spirit... works in us, individually and collectively. We receive the Spirit of God in Baptism.

We celebrate the Holy Eucharist and the Lord will be present with us, but only through the invocation and the calling down of the Holy Spirit. The Holy Spirit moves within every corner of the Church... from the election of a pope... to the sins that are forgiven in little confessionals throughout the world. The Spirit of God is alive and breathing every time you and I pray. Every time we love... every time we forgive... every time we do a noble deed the spirit of God moves upon the land.

Let us take a moment... together... in the depths of our heart to prove to one another that the Holy Spirit moves among us. Say this aloud with me:

Jesus Christ is Lord.

Say it again.

Jesus Christ is Lord.

Say it one more time.

Jesus Christ is Lord.

No one can say, "Jesus is Lord," except by the Holy Spirit.

No one can say, "Jesus Christ is Lord," unless moved by the Spirit of God to do so.

It is also fitting on this Pentecost Sunday to honor and to give thanks to a marvelous group of women: the Sisters of Providence.

The Sisters of Providence are Sisters who gave their lives to Catholic education.... Sisters who gave their lives to Christ through Catholic education. My heavens... how the Spirit of God used them!

Father Andrew Greeley, in a study on the Church, asserted that the greatest contribution of the Church, in the United States, to the Church universal, was the parochial school system- particularly as it was known in the forties and fifties. The parochial school system was a marvelous contribution, not only to the Church universal, but to American society as well. The contribution of the Sisters of Providence to the parochial school system was one of love and one of tremendous dedication. In so many ways the Sisters of Providence were the lesson.

The Sisters of Providence spoke not only through words, but also by who they were... and by who they are. The Sisters spoke of what it meant to be the Church and what it meant to be a teacher: one who served. The contribution made by the Sisters of Providence is one that only God will ever be able to fully repay.

There is a plaque affixed to the back wall of Saint Francis Xavier, dedicated to the Sisters of Providence. It reads, "Before we were here as a parish, you were here."

In that spirit I am mindful of little Sister Marie, who walked to Saint Francis Xavier, in the city of Winooski, from North Avenue, in Burlington, every day, to teach little children about their church. Her's is a story similar to that of Mother Francis Ward, who lived in Cleveland, Ohio.

Mother Francis Ward walked to mass through a raging snow storm, one violent winter day, though ravaged by a terrible fever. She was determined never to miss mass and, on that day, was determined to have breakfast with a young priest named Louis DeGoesbriand. Louis DeGoesbriand eventually became the first Bishop of the Diocese of Burlington. He never forgot the dedication and deep faith of Mother Francis Ward.

Sisters of Providence, more than ever we need your spirit. We need your prayers. We need your example. The Spirit of God breathes. It is alive. The Holy Spirit is with His Church. It moves upon us in many ways and with many forms: one of which is through the Sisters of Providence.

For the wonderful, wonderful example you set for all of us... for the many years of dedication and service... dear Sisters of Providence... from the bottom of our hearts... we thank you.

Fr. Lavalley

He will come again in glory to judge the living and the dead, and His kingdom will have no end...

A note from the Scribe

I was reclining in bed one lazy midwinter afternoon, when my alarm clock inconveniently began signaling the end of my usual midday nap. The radio was tuned to WDEV-FM, broadcasting over the mountain somewhere east of Bristol, in Warren, Vermont. I was languishing somewhere between asleep and awake when the melody and the words of a song performed by the Moody Blues coaxed me into a state of unwelcome lucidity.

> I know you're out there somewhere,
> Somewhere, somewhere.
> I know I'll find you somehow,
> Somehow, somehow.
> And somehow I'll return again to you.

The song I heard that day was a song I had heard many times before and many years earlier; one of many popular songs emanating from the stereo speakers of a television set in a tavern, Nutini's Supper Club, in the Upper Peninsula of Michigan, during the heyday of VH-1's popularity.

> The mist is lifting slowly,
> I can see the way ahead.
> And I've left behind the empty streets
> That once inspired my life.
> And the strength of the emotion,
> Is like thunder in the air.

Cos' the promise that we made each other,
Haunts me to the end.

The song, entitled *I Know You're Out There Somewhere*, was written, composed, and sung by the Moody Blues. I recall enjoying its melody back in the day, but I never gave its lyrics much attention. On this particular lazy afternoon, however, the words of the artist spoke to me in a way they had never done before... for it seemed to me as though the song's composer was calling out to our God... to our Lord and Savior. There was a yearning in the tone and a determination in the words.

I know you're out there somewhere,
Somewhere, somewhere.
I know you're out there somewhere,
Somewhere you can hear my voice.
I know I'll find you somehow,
Somehow, somehow.
I know I'll find you somehow,
And somehow I'll return again to you.

Short of learning of the artist's muse from the mouth of the composer, I have no way of knowing whether or not his intention was a calling-out to our Lord. But this is an example of how one's perception of life... and of the things of one's life... change when one accepts Jesus Christ as Lord and Savior and can say with sincerity and intimacy, "Jesus, I love you."

The secret of your beauty,
And the mystery of your soul,
I've been searching for in everyone I meet.
And the times I've been mistaken,
It's impossible to say.
And the grass is growing underneath our feet.

I know you're out there somewhere,
Somewhere, somewhere.
I know you're out there somewhere,
Somewhere you can hear my voice.
I know I'll find you somehow,
Somehow, somehow.

I know I'll find you somehow,
And somehow I'll return again to you.

The words that I remember,
From my childhood still are true.
There are none so blind,
As those who will not see.
And to those who lack the courage,
Who say it's dangerous to try,
Well they just don't know,
That love eternal will not be denied.

Love eternal... love's first kiss... all of the things Father Lavalley speaks of often... on so many occasions... with conviction... with intimate knowledge... with uncanny and unwavering confidence. Well, you get the point...

Several years ago, I received an e-mail from a former colleague. This particular e-mail was one of those internet "comet" e-mails. You know the kind... one in which the recipient is asked to answer questions and, then, to forward the e-mail onward to ten other e-mail recipients. As is usually the case with such e-mails, this e-mail also directed the recipient to send a copy of his or her responses back to the person from whom the e-mail was received.

For me, personally, the e-mail was a curious one, in that, two of the ten questions posed were: *1). If you could choose anyone in the world, who is the one person with whom you would most want to dine? and, 2). If you could choose anyone in the world, who is the one person with whom you would least want to dine?*

I peeked at the responses that came before my impending ones and was quietly amused to discover that the previous responders listed Jesus Christ as the one person with whom they would most like to dine, and someone evil like... Hitler or Pol Pot or Jeffrey Dahmer... as persons with whom they would least want to dine.

I answered the questions, selected ten unsuspecting recipients from my e-mail address book, hit the "Send" button, and sent the internet comet hurtling off into cyberspace. Within several days, copies of emails containing responses by my e-mail addressees began landing in my "Inbox".

For the most part the responses were fairly standard. Favorite colors were blues, reds, and greens. Favorite foods were burgers, pizzas, and grilled cheese sandwiches. And when it came to the two questions I found to be personally thought-provoking...there were those who also wished to dine with Jesus Christ... some wished to dine with rock stars... or movie stars. Predictably... there were also those who wished not to dine with Hitler... Pol Pot... etc...

But one copy of an e-mail I received really stood out from all the rest. I suppose two reasons for its prominence was: the person from whom it was returned, and the nature of the responses.

To the question ...*If you could choose anyone in the world... who is the one person with whom you would most want to dine...* I do not, at this time, recall the given response. But to the question ...*If you could choose anyone in the world... who is the one person with whom you would least want to dine...* the response given was: A preacher.

That response troubled me greatly.

Now... I realize the original e-mail was probably an exercise in frivolity on the part of some bored internet surfer. But... whereas, I had been buoyed by many of the responses to this particular exercise in frivolity, for they appeared to offer a tiny window into the lives of people with whom I am associated or acquainted... and the responses in the majority of instances were indicative of the good character I had come to believe was found in those people... there, in that one response, I felt an uneasiness settle upon my soul.

Of all of the evil that exists in this world... of all of the wickedness and inequity and vileness that is present in this world... it was striking to me that, on balance, one of my acquaintances would abhor the thought of breaking bread with one of God's children who has chosen to spend his or her life spreading the "Good News". This is, after all, what a preacher does. Why would someone find such a calling abhorrent?

These days I still find myself scratching my head, trying to make sense of the response given by that one person.

Much is made nowadays of the instances of corruption and perversion that has been found to exist in some corners of our religious institutions. To be sure... such vileness is to be scorned and properly reconciled, but these days far too many cast a gleeful eye upon such unfortunate affairs and are so, so eager to herald the decline of our society's religious pillars. It gives one pause to wonder.

Corruption exists within **all** institutions touched by man's hand, because man, himself, is invariably corrupt. Such does not make the basis of our faith... the core of our belief... corrupt. Our corruptibility as humans, born of original sin, makes corruption an inevitable facet of the human experience. And while corruption, particularly in those with whom we have placed our utmost trust and have been woefully deceived, is a condition to be rightfully chastised... each of us can look into our heart and know that there have been times in our life when we have corrupted our self.

I entered the life of Father Richard G. Lavalley one Sunday in the fall of '99. I have no logical explanation for how the change that came upon me... came upon me. I recall sitting in a pew at Saint Francis... fourth row from the front... seat closest to the left side of the center aisle... and Father Lavalley was speaking, as he so eloquently does, of Jesus... and of love... and of forgiveness... and of compassion... and of all the things that can be found on any one page in this book... when something came upon me.

I have searched for many years to fully describe the transformation I felt take hold of me on that Sunday... on that autumn day in 1999. The closest I have ever been able to come is to suggest that something entered me very deeply and settled between my physical self and my spiritual being- separating one from the other.

At long last I felt unencumbered to fully embrace our Lord and Savior Jesus Christ. I felt free to experience the wisdom of His teaching... free to experience the deep sorrow of His crucifixion... free to experience the mystery of His resurrection... free to experience the joy of His salvation... free to speak of Him... and free to speak with Him as though He were beside me every minute of every hour of every day.

At long last I felt free to love Him... and in turn, free to love others with an unselfish, abiding, spiritual love.

I credit Father Lavalley for my journey to the feet of Christ... for it was Father Lavalley who illuminated the pathway for my heart to follow.

It bears repeating that Father Lavalley is a man of deep spiritual substance. He is a man possessive of a deep, abiding love for the people whom he serves... for his blessed calling to the priesthood... for everything that is Jesus Christ and is of Jesus Christ. Father Lavalley is a teacher to his people... a mentor to those who thirst for his wisdom. Father Lavalley is a conscience for those who would go astray. He is a comforting shoulder... a steadying hand for those in despair. And you know something else...?

Father Lavalley is every bit as good as Father Bombardier was when it comes to cracking wise!

D.B. Prehoda

I know you're out there somewhere,
Somewhere, somewhere.
I know you're out there somewhere,
Somewhere you can hear my voice.
I know I'll find you somehow,
Somehow, somehow.
I know I'll find you somehow,
And somehow I'll return again to you.

Joannes Paulus PP. II

John Paul II

Karol Jozef Wojtyla was born on May 18, 1920, in Wadowice, Poland, a small city near Krakow. He was the second son of two children born to Karol Wojtyla Sr., and Emilia Kaczorowska Wojtyla. His father was a retired army officer and a tailor. His mother was a schoolteacher.

During his childhood, Karol experienced many hardships. His mother and his brother, Edmund, died when he was still quite young. His father died in 1941, when Karol was twenty years of age.

As a teenager, Karol enjoyed religion, poetry, and theater. In 1938, he enrolled at Krakow's Jagiellonian University to study literature and philosophy. The university was closed in 1939, however, by the Nazi's, who occupied Poland at that time. Karol was forced to work in a quarry and a chemical factory, in order to earn a living and to avoid deportation to Germany. During those turbulent years of German occupation Karol helped set up an underground university and the clandestine Rhapsodic Theater.

In 1942, Karol responded to the sacred calling of the priesthood, and began his religious education at the clandestine seminary of Krakow. When World War II ended Karol resumed his studies at the major seminary of Krakow, and at the Faculty of Theology of Jagiellonian University. Karol was ordained as a priest on November 01, 1946. He began life anew as Father Wojtyla. His religious education continued at Rome's Angelicum University.

Upon his return to Poland, from Rome, Father Wojtyla became the vicar of various parishes in Krakow, as well as, the chaplain for university students. In 1951, Father Wojtyla resumed his studies of philosophy and theology, and eventually became a professor of moral theology and social ethics at the major seminary of Krakow, and in the Faculty of Theology of Lublin Catholic University.

Pope Pius XII appointed Father Wojtyla to the position of Auxiliary Bishop of Krakow, in 1958. In 1964, Father Wojtyla was nominated Archbishop of Krakow by Pope Paul VI, and was made a Cardinal by Pope Paul VI, in 1967.

Cardinal Wojtyla was one of the youngest cardinals in the Church. He was a moderate reformer with a strategy that honored the beliefs and traditions of Catholicism while, at the same time, accommodating the Communist government of Poland.

On October 16, 1978, Cardinal Wojtyla was chosen by the Sacred College of Cardinals, as the next Pope. He took the name John Paul II, and became the first Slavic Pope. He immediately embarked on a journey of restoring the Catholic Church to its traditional, conservative roots.

Pope John Paul II was the youngest Pope in one hundred and thirty-two years. He was a divine leader with a keen intellect, deep compassion, and an abiding spirituality. He was welcomed by Catholics and non-Catholics the world over. Pope John Paul II is credited for his moral-boosting trips to numerous countries. He is known for his political activism- most notably for helping to defeat European Communism. He defended human rights, worldwide. He was the most traveled Pope in history; he frequently used the media and technology to communicate issues related to moral, ethical, and global affairs. Ultimately, Pope John Paul II believed that prayer and faith could make people happy and could change the world.

Information Source: www.vatican.va

Joannes Paulus PP. II

A Tribute to John Paul II

A reading from the Book of Wisdom:

The souls of the just are in the hand of God and no torment shall touch them. They seemed in view of the foolish to be dead and their passing away was thought an affliction and their going forth from us utter destruction, but they are in peace. For if before men, indeed, they be punished, yet is their hope full of immortality. Chastised a little they shall be greatly blessed, because God tried them and found them worthy of himself. As gold in a furnace he proved them and as sacrificial offerings he took them to himself. In the time of their visitation they shall shine and shall dart about as sparks through stubble. They shall judge nations and rule over peoples and the Lord shall be their king forever. Those who trust in him shall understand truth and the faithful shall abide with him in love, because grace and mercy are with his holy ones and his care is with his elect.

A reading from the Letter of Paul to the Romans:

Are you not aware that we who were baptized into Christ Jesus were baptized into his death. Through baptism into his death we were buried with him so that just as Christ was raised from the dead by the glory of the Father we too might live a new life. If we have been united with him through likeness to his death so shall we be through a like resurrection, this we know. Our old self was crucified with him so that the sinful body might be destroyed and we might be slaves to sin no longer. A man who is dead has been freed from sin. If we have died with Christ we believe that we are also to live with him. We know that Christ once raised from the dead will never die again. Death has no more power over him.

A reading from the holy Gospel according to Matthew:

When Jesus came to the neighborhood of Caesarea Philippi, he asked his disciples this question, "Who do people say that the Son of Man is?" They replied, "Some say John the Baptist, others Elijah, still others Jeremiah or one of the prophets." "And you," he said to them. "Who do you say that I am?" "You are the Messiah," Simon Peter answered. "The Son of the living God." Jesus replied, "Blessed are you, Simon son of Jonah! No mere man has revealed this to you, but my heavenly Father. I, for my part, declare to you, you are rock and on this rock I will build my church and the jaws of death shall not prevail against it. I will entrust to you the keys of the kingdom of heaven. Whatever you declare bound on earth shall be bound in heaven. And whatever you declare loosed on earth shall be loosed in heaven." Then, he strictly ordered his disciples not to tell anyone that he was the Messiah.

Let us take this occasion to talk a little bit about the day of the passing of our Holy Father, John Paul II. The words of the Gospel according to Matthew go to the heart of our faith. *"Thou art Peter, and on this rock I will build my church, and the gates of hell will never prevail against it."*

"And behold, I am with you all days, even to the ends of the earth."

I watched much of the ceremony leading up to the internment of our Holy Father, John Paul II, on the television. And, as the Holy Father was laying in state, I was struck by the hundreds of thousands of people who passed by... who waited in line for hours on end for a brief glance at the mortal remains of him. But at one point, while I was watching the television coverage, it occurred to me that not everyone was seeing the same thing... not everyone was looking at the same thing... not everyone was arriving with the same agenda. Oh... I believe all of the agendas were good... but they were not the same agenda. Some people were in Rome, viewing the remains of our Holy Father, because that is what everyone else was doing. Some people were in Rome, viewing the remains of our Holy Father, because they were caught up in the frenzy of the moment. Some people were in Rome, viewing the remains of our Holy Father, because it was a magnificently, marvelously, spectacular event.

Some were there to honor a man, who was an advocate of life and an enemy to war. Some were there to honor a man, who was a great peacemaker and a humanitarian. Some were there to honor a man, who held out his hands and opened his heart to the oppressed. Some were there to honor a man, who had respect for all human beings, whether they were of his faith or of another. Some were there to honor a man, who was determined, who was a man of character. Some were there to honor a man, who absolutely loved children. Some were there to honor a man, who knew how to steer the ark of Peter. Some were there to honor a man, who taught us how to live... and some were there to honor a man, who taught us how to die.

All of those reasons for being there are wonderful. They are beautiful reasons. But others were gathered in that place for the very same reason we are gathered together, today.

We are the Church.

That is who we are.

We are the Church, and we witnessed all of those things that everyone else witnessed, but we observed something else.

We saw our Holy Father.

You and I saw the Vicar of Christ on earth.

You and I saw the successor to Saint Peter.

We saw a man, who steered the boat and whose feet filled the shoes of the Fisherman for twenty-six years. We saw a Holy Father, who had a wonderful heart, a marvelous mind, and arms that could embrace an entire world. The entire world was his church. And we celebrate the passing of John Paul II by saying, "Holy Father, we love you and we are grateful to God for the gift of you. You taught us so much."

Here is my favorite story of John Paul II. It is not one of the "big" stories. It is a small story, but somehow this story out of all of the others impressed me the most.

When the Holy Father traveled to New York City... I believe it was his first visit to the United States... he was not feeling well. He was tired from traveling and from the fullness of that first day in the U.S. In the middle of the night the Vatican needed to reach him. His aides went to his bedroom, where he was billeted in the rectory of Saint Patrick's Cathedral, but the Holy Father was not there. Not knowing the whereabouts of the Holy Father caused great concern and panic among his security personnel. An immediate search for John Paul II ensued.

All was well. He was found a short while later in the private chapel of Saint Patrick's Cathedral. He was in the company of the Holy Eucharist. In the middle of the night the Holy Father was praying. He was tired and frayed from his travel and his engagements, yet he knew where the source of his strength could be found. He knew from whence his power came. He knew who he was... and he knew who Jesus was. He knew that the source of his strength was the Holy Eucharist. He knew that without the Holy Eucharist, he was nothing.

Could it be any more fitting that the death of John Paul II occurred during the year proclaimed by the Church as the year of the Holy Eucharist?

So... even in our mourning of the passing of the Holy Father we celebrate the Holy Eucharist, because the Church goes on. Popes will come and popes will go... but the Church will go on... and on... and on. It is beautiful. It is wonderful. It is mysterious. The light of the Holy Eucharist continues to burn.

And behold, I am with you all days...

The encyclical letter on the Holy Eucharist says it all:

"The heart of the Church is the Holy Eucharist."

The heart of the Church is the Holy Eucharist.

And so... John Paul II... Karol Jozef Wojtyla... son of Karol Wojtyla and Emilia Kaczorowska Wojtyla has traveled home to be reunited with the Father, and with the Son, and with the Holy Spirit.

Amen

Fr. Lavalley